Chinese Consumers in a New Era

As a newcomer to tourism, China has amazed the world with its rapid growth of inbound, outbound, and domestic tourism. Tourists from the Greater China area (Mainland, Hong Kong, Macao, and Taiwan) are well positioned to change the world's tourism landscape. Influence of China in the global tourism arena will be even more significant with the realization of WTO's vision of Mainland China as a top world tourism destination and tourist-generating country by 2020. The preeminent role of Chinese travellers in the social space of tourism has stimulated much interest in understanding their behaviors and psychology in various tourism settings. The chapters in this collection investigate different aspects of Chinese consumer behaviors and psychology in tourism settings.

This book was originally published as a special issue of the *Journal of China Tourism Research*.

Kam Hung is an assistant professor at the School of Hotel and Tourism Management of The Hong Kong Polytechnic University, Hong Kong. She received her Master's and Ph.D degrees from Texas A&M University, USA. Her research interests include tourism marketing, tourist behavior and psychology, senior travel, and cruise tourism.

Xiang (Robert) Li is an associate professor at the School of Hotel, Restaurant, and Tourism Management, University of South Carolina, USA. His research mainly focuses on destination marketing and tourist behavior, with special emphasis on international destination branding, customer loyalty, and tourism in Asia.

Chinese Consumers in a New Era

Their Travel Behaviors and Psychology

Edited by
Kam Hung and Xiang (Robert) Li

LONDON AND NEW YORK

First published 2015 by Routledge

2 Park Square, Milton Park, Abingdon, Oxon, OX14 4RN
605 Third Avenue, New York, NY 10017

Routledge is an imprint of the Taylor & Francis Group, an informa business

First issued in paperback 2020

British Library Cataloguing in Publication Data
A catalogue record for this book is available from the British Library

ISBN13: 978-1-138-80185-1 (hbk)
ISBN13: 978-0-367-73994-2 (pbk)

Typeset in Times New Roman
by RefineCatch Limited, Bungay, Suffolk

Publisher's Note
The publisher accepts responsibility for any inconsistencies that may have
arisen during the conversion of this book from journal articles to book chapters,
namely the possible inclusion of journal terminology.

Disclaimer
Every effort has been made to contact copyright holders for their permission to
reprint material in this book. The publishers would be grateful to hear from any
copyright holder who is not here acknowledged and will undertake to rectify
any errors or omissions in future editions of this book.

Contents

Citation Information vii

Introduction 1
Kam Hung and Xiang (Robert) Li

1. Exploring Chinese Outbound Tourism Motivation Using Means–End Chains: A Conceptual Model 3
Shan Jiang, Noel Scott, Peiyi Ding and Tony Tongqian Zou

2. Comparing Mainland Chinese Tourists' Satisfaction With Hong Kong and the UK Using Tourist Satisfaction Index 17
Gang Li, Haiyan Song, Jason Li Chen and Doris Chenguang Wu

3. Annoying Tourist Behaviors: Perspectives of Hosts and Tourists in Macao 39
Kim Ieng Loi and Philip L. Pearce

4. An Empirical Study of Anticipated and Perceived Discrimination of Mainland Chinese Tourists in Hong Kong: The Role of Intercultural Competence 61
Ben Haobin Ye, Hanqin Qiu Zhang and Peter P. Yuen

5. From Destination Image to Destination Loyalty: Evidence From Recreation Farms in Taiwan 75
Chyong-Ru Liu, Wei-Rong Lin and Yao-Chin Wang

6. Selection of Outbound Package Tours: The Case of Senior Citizens in Hong Kong 94
Louisa Yee-Sum Lee, Henry Tsai, Nelson K. F. Tsang and Ada S. Y. Lo

Index 113

Citation Information

The chapters in this book were originally published in the *Journal of China Tourism Research*, volume 8, issue 4 (December 2012). When citing this material, please use the original page numbering for each article, as follows:

Introduction
Guest Editor's Note
Kam Hung and Xiang (Robert) Li
Journal of China Tourism Research, volume 8, issue 4 (December 2012) pp. 357–358

Chapter 1
Exploring Chinese Outbound Tourism Motivation Using Means–End Chains: A Conceptual Model
Shan Jiang, Noel Scott, Peiyi Ding and Tony Tongqian Zou
Journal of China Tourism Research, volume 8, issue 4 (December 2012) pp. 359–372

Chapter 2
Comparing Mainland Chinese Tourists' Satisfaction With Hong Kong and the UK Using Tourist Satisfaction Index
Gang Li, Haiyan Song, Jason Li Chen and Doris Chenguang Wu
Journal of China Tourism Research, volume 8, issue 4 (December 2012) pp. 373–394

Chapter 3
Annoying Tourist Behaviors: Perspectives of Hosts and Tourists in Macao
Kim Ieng Loi and Philip L. Pearce
Journal of China Tourism Research, volume 8, issue 4 (December 2012) pp. 395–416

Chapter 4
An Empirical Study of Anticipated and Perceived Discrimination of Mainland Chinese Tourists in Hong Kong: The Role of Intercultural Competence
Ben Haobin Ye, Hanqin Qiu Zhang and Peter P. Yuen
Journal of China Tourism Research, volume 8, issue 4 (December 2012) pp. 417–430

Chapter 5
From Destination Image to Destination Loyalty: Evidence From Recreation Farms in Taiwan
Chyong-Ru Liu, Wei-Rong Lin and Yao-Chin Wang
Journal of China Tourism Research, volume 8, issue 4 (December 2012) pp. 431–449

Chapter 6

Selection of Outbound Package Tours: The Case of Senior Citizens in Hong Kong
Louisa Yee-Sum Lee, Henry Tsai, Nelson K. F. Tsang and Ada S. Y. Lo
Journal of China Tourism Research, volume 8, issue 4 (December 2012) pp. 450–468

Please direct any queries you may have about the citations to
clsuk.permissions@cengage.com

Introduction

As a newcomer to tourism, China has amazed the world with its rapid growth of inbound, outbound, and domestic tourism. Tourists from the Greater China area (Mainland, Hong Kong, Macao, and Taiwan) are well positioned to change the world's tourism landscape. China's influence in the global tourism arena will be even more significant with the realization of the World Tourism Organization's vision of Mainland China as a top world tourism destination and tourist-generating country by 2020. The preeminent role of Chinese travelers in the social space of tourism has stimulated much interest in understanding their behaviors and psychology in various tourism settings.

This special issue features six articles that investigate different aspects of Chinese consumer behaviors and psychology in tourism settings. Shan Jiang, Noel Scott, Peiyi Ding, and Tony Tongqian Zou develop a conceptual model based on the means–end chain theory to understand the travel motivation of Chinese outbound tourists. Gang Li, Haiyan Song, Jason Li Chen, and Doris Chenguang Wu compare Mainland Chinese tourists' satisfaction level with Hong Kong and the UK through a Tourist Satisfaction Index (TSI) approach. Kim Ieng Loi and Philip L. Pearce examine the undesirable behaviors of Chinese tourists in Macao from the perspectives of both tourists and local residents. Ben Haobin Ye, Hanqin Qiu Zhang, and Peter P. Yuen identify key factors affecting Chinese tourists' level of anticipated and perceived discrimination. Chyong-Ru Liu, Wei-Rong Lin, and Yao-Chin Wang empirically test the relationships among destination image, self-congruity, destination personality, and destination loyalty in Taiwan in an effort to build a visitors' behavior model. Finally, Louisa Yee-Sum Lee, Henry Tsai, Nelson K. F. Tsang, and Ada S. Y. Lo investigate the perceived importance and performance of key attributes related to outbound package tours among Hong Kong senior citizens.

Current tourist behavior studies worldwide are clearly dominated by Western research tradition, though researchers have repeatedly voiced their concerns about the limitations and incommensurability issue when applying the Western research paradigm to non-Western contexts (Iwasaki, Nishino, Onda, & Bowling, 2007; Sheth, 2011). Thus, understanding non-Western consumer behavior could be a critical step toward breaking free from potential Western research bias and embracing a new, truly "globalized" researcher paradigm. Though this special issue only serves as the tip of the iceberg in understanding Chinese traveler behavior and mindsets, it is our hope that such an endeavor will continue and generate more discussion on this topic in both scholarly and practitioner communities.

Kam Hung
Xiang (Robert) Li
Guest Editors

References

Iwasaki, Y., Nishino, H., Onda, T., & Bowling, C. (2007). Leisure research in a global world: Time to reverse the Western domination in leisure research? *Leisure Sciences, 29*(1), 113–117.

Sheth, J. N. (2011). Impact of emerging markets on marketing: Rethinking existing perspectives and practices. *Journal of Marketing, 75*(4), 166–182.

Exploring Chinese Outbound Tourism Motivation Using Means–End Chains: A Conceptual Model

通过"手段目的链"研究中国出境旅游者动机：一个概念模型的提出

SHAN JIANG
NOEL SCOTT
PEIYI DING
TONY TONGQIAN ZOU

Over the last decade, the Chinese outbound tourism market has experienced rapid development, and understanding the tourism motivations of this growth market is critical to understanding their decision-making processes and tourism behaviors. By reviewing the literature on tourism motivations and analyzing the limitations in this research area, this theoretical article develops a conceptual model based on means–end chain (MEC) theory to study the tourism motivations of Chinese outbound tourists and discusses the associated laddering technique required by the MEC theory. It is argued that exploring tourism motivation with the MEC theory will make both theoretical and methodological contributions to tourism motivation research, as well as provide more meaningful information for understanding Chinese outbound tourists.

过去的二十年，中国出境旅游市场经历了迅猛的发展。研究此市场人群的旅游动机，对了解其旅游决策过程和旅游行为是至关重要的。本文通过对旅游动机文献的综述，分析了此研究领域存在的不足，同时通过应用"手段目的链"理论，提出了一个概念模型来研究中国出境旅游者动机，并探讨了"手段目的链"相联系的"梯式递进"研究方法。此文论证了在理论层面和研究方法层面，"手段目的链"理论研究旅游动机的重要作用，并指出此方法能够为了解中国出境旅游者提供更多有价值的信息。

关键词：中国出境市场，旅游动机，手段目的链理论

Shan Jiang is a PhD candidate in the School of Tourism at The University of Queensland, St. Lucia, Queensland, Australia.

Noel Scott is Associate Professor in the School of Tourism at The University of Queensland, St. Lucia, Queensland, Australia.

Peiyi Ding is a business manager in the Tourism Confucius Institute at Griffith University, Queensland, Australia.

Tony Tongqian Zou is a Professor in the School of Tourism Management at Beijing International Studies University, China.

Background

Leisure travel for Chinese people was almost nonexistent until 1979, but today China's tourism industry is among the fastest-growing sector of its economy. The country's gross domestic product grew from 486 billion yuan (or US$58 billion) in 1981 to 47,156 billion yuan (or US$7,485 billion) in 2011, at an average growth rate of nearly 10% (National Bureau of Statistics of China, n.d.). This growth in tourism demand within China is the result of economic growth, and a large middle-class population with strong purchasing power is emerging in China, especially in major cities such as Beijing and Shanghai. It has been observed in recent years that an increasing proportion of urban household income has been allocated to tourism (Shao, 2012); visa applications have become easier, online reservations are growing, and customer choice has become more Westernized (Tse & Hobson, 2008). As a result, the Chinese outbound tourism market has also experienced rapid development over the last decade (Figure 1). It was reported that China has become a rapidly growing market for outbound tourism in Asia, and many countries even regard it as the source of hope for economic recovery (World Tourism Organization [WTO], 2003).

China is very different from many countries due to its unique culture and language. Their different habits and outlooks have a great impact on Chinese people's choice of destination and their tourism motivations. Though currently most tourists join group tours and visit several countries in one trip, independent travel and mono-destination holidays are emerging as a new trend for Chinese outbound tourism (China Tourism Association, 2010). It was also found that Chinese travelers are willing to spend large amounts of money during their travels (WTO, 2003). In order to explore China's outbound tourism market, it is necessary to understand the distinguishing features and characteristics of Chinese consumers to develop tourist products to meet their needs and to conduct marketing and promotion activities. Therefore, exploring the travel motivation of Chinese outbound tourists is an important topic for both tourism researchers and destination marketers, who are eager to understand Chinese tourists' psychological and cultural characteristics.

In the field of tourism research, it is widely accepted that tourism motivation research is an area still fraught with theoretical problems and it is still difficult to

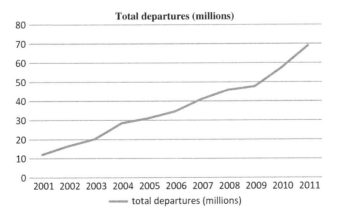

Figure 1. Chinese outbound departures, 2001–2011. Adapted from *China Tourism Industry Statistics Bulletin* (color figure available online).

measure unobservable parameters (Dann, Nash, & Pearce, 1988; Hsu & Huang, 2008; Jafari, 1987; Jamal & Lee, 2003; Kluin & Lehto, 2012; Pearce & Lee, 2005). This theoretical article (a) critically reviews mainstream motivation theories to identify their advantages and limitations; (b) introduces means–end chain (MEC) theory from the marketing research field as a new approach to explore tourism motivation by developing a conceptual model in the context of Chinese outbound travel market; and (c) discusses the laddering technique as a means to conducting MEC research.

A Review of Tourism Motivation Theories

Tourism motivation is a critical explanatory factor in discovering and understanding tourists' decision-making processes and behaviors and examining why people travel. However, it is also a very complex research area, and numerous theoretical approaches have been adopted (Crompton, 1979; Uysal & Hagan, 1993). According to psychologists, *motivation* is "the concept we use when we describe the forces acting on or within an organism to initiate and direct behaviour" (Petri & Govern, 2004, p. 16). In the field of tourism, *tourism motivation* was defined by Dann (1981) as "a meaningful state of mind which adequately disposes an actor or group of actors to travel, and which is subsequently interpretable by others as a valid explanation for such a decision" (p. 205). The following is a critical review of a number of main theories in tourism motivation, which includes Plog's psychocentric–allocentric model (Plog, 1974, 2001), Iso-Ahola's escaping and seeking theory (Iso-Ahola, 1982; Mannell & Iso-Ahola, 1987), Dann's push and pull theory (Dann, 1977), Pearce's travel career pattern (Pearce, 2005), and Fodness's function theory (Fodness, 1994).

Psychocentric–Allocentric Model

Plog (1974) introduced a tourist psychographics system based on the belief that tourists' travel patterns and preferences are determined by their personality characteristics. His model has been criticized as tautological (Braun, 1989) and explaining nothing (Gnoth, 1997). Plog later revised and refined his model and supported it with data from the annual American Traveller Survey (Plog, 2001, 2002). According to Plog (2001), the general population can be grouped into five types of people, varying from allocentric, to near venture, mid-centric, near dependable, and psychocentric. Allocentric people are intellectually curious and want to explore the world, make decisions quickly and easily, and are more likely to choose new destinations. On the other hand, psychocentric people are restrictive in spending discretionary income and prefer more popular, well-known brands of consumer products and destinations. Plog (2001) asserted that destinations could be placed on the psychographic curve, based on the types of people who visit there the most. Changes in the type of people attracted to a destination based on their personality could help to explain why destinations rise and fall in popularity. Some scholars regarded this model as not a valid proxy to predict or describe life cycle evolution because it uses the psychographic profile of visitors alone (McKercher, 2005) and is not realistic (Chen, Mak, & McKercher, 2011). Moreover, the model as a psychographic tool is limited because it does not consider multiple-motivated behaviors and is unable to explain why different types of tourists visit a single destination.

Escaping and Seeking Theory

Iso Ahola and Mannell developed a social psychological model of tourism motivation (SPMTM; Iso-Ahola, 1982; Mannell & Iso-Ahola, 1987). The SPMTM model suggests that tourism motivation can be categorized into four types: seeking personal rewards, seeking interpersonal rewards, escaping personal environment, and escaping interpersonal environment (Mannell & Iso-Ahola, 1987). The model suggests that seeking and escaping are both part of tourism motivation. The escaping and seeking theory has provided a new perspective to explore travel motivation within the context of leisure and social environment, and it was later supported by other studies (Dunn Ross & Iso-Ahola, 1991; Snepenger, King, Marshall, & Uysal, 2006). However, one criticism of the theory is that it does not explain the underlying reason for escape as the tourism motivation (Jamal & Lee, 2003) and hence fails to address the processes and means by which certain motivations arise rather than others. Second is that Iso-Ahola's (1982) model does not provide explicit insights into the structure or content of those needs, and it is not a strong predictive tool because it assumes that all people equally share one common need that can be satisfied by intrinsic or extrinsic rewards (White & Thompson, 2009). Thirdly, Iso-Ahola (1982) regarded motivation as "purely a psychological concept" (p. 257), and it is arguable that travel motivation is a part of, or one form of, leisure motivation (Jamal & Lee, 2003). It is generally considered that tourism and leisure motivation overlap to some degree, but there are also many differences between these two fields, and they cannot be studied as one phenomenon. Travel motivation is only partly similar to that found in the leisure domain and is considered worthy of independent theory building (Pearce, 1993).

Push and Pull Theory

Push and pull factors were first proposed by Dann in 1977 and have been widely adopted in tourism research studies (Hsu & Huang, 2008). According to Dann (1981), *pull factors* are the specific attractions that induce tourists to visit a particular destination rather than another once the decision to undertake a trip has been made (e.g., heritage and culture, beaches, friendly people, etc.), and *push factors* are internally generated drives that cause the tourist to search for signs in objects, situations, and events that contain the promise of reducing prevalent drives. Push and pull theory is widely used in tourism motivation research (i.e., Crompton, 1979; Jang & Wu, 2006; Kozak, 2002; Yuan & McDonald, 1990).

However, a number of limitations of this theory have been highlighted. First of all, it is not clear in this theory how to define the two factors in terms of their dimensional levels. For example, in Crompton's study (1979), *novelty* and *education* as pull factors, along with push factors such as *escape from routine*, *self-discovery*, *relaxation*, *improve family relationships*, and *facilitate social interaction* could be regarded as benefits received from tourism. The push factors of *prestige* and *regression* are, however, at a deeper level of motivation and are closer to the values of *social reorganization* and *freedom* (Rokeach, 1973). In the work of Yuan and McDonald (1990), again, prestige is regarded as one push factor among other beneficial motivations. However, prestige is not only a benefit but is more of an instrumental value motivation directed toward social recognition as the terminal value.

In addition, the theory fails to clearly describe how these motivations relate to each other or how push and pull factors work together to generate tourism motivation and to what degree each factor acts to motivate. According to Dann (1977), "while a specific resort may hold a number of attractions for the potential tourist, his actual decision to visit such a destination is consequent on his prior need for travel" (p. 186). Hence, push factors are logically regarded as the antecedent of pull factors. As an example, Jang and Wu (2006) applied the push and pull conceptual framework and used factor analyses to study the tourism motivation of Taiwanese tourists. In this study, "I think that the kind of accommodation that you get on a trip is important" was regarded as a push factor but, arguably, "the kind of accommodation" is a destination attribute. Moreover, it is doubtful that this item should be included in a push factor called *self-esteem* without exploring this further with the respondents. As a result, in this study more specific motivations for choice of a certain kind of accommodation are ignored and are assumed to be included in the self-esteem–related motivation. Indeed, push and pull factors are generated using factor analysis and are interpreted by analysts based on the analyst's understanding of the data. As a result, it is doubtful without confirming these underlying reasons with respondents that push and pull factors adequately reflect travelers' motivations. Instead, they may be artefacts of the analyst's imperfect understanding of the data.

Furthermore, push and pull factors should not be treated as operating entirely independently of each other (Crompton, 1979), and the relationship between push and pull factors should be discussed because pull factors both respond to and reinforce push factors (Dann, 1981). Though several studies have investigated the relationship between push and pull factors (i.e., Chul Oh, Uysal, & Weaver, 1995; Kim & Lee, 2002; Uysal & Jurowski, 1994), their results are limited in that (a) the results cannot provide more information on what kind of relationship there is and how one factor is related to another; that is, is there a causal relationship between the two factors, or is there only a correlation with the other? (b) the push and pull items do not consider all possible dimensions of motivation (Chul Oh et al., 1995), which means that although these two factors are related, there may be other stronger relationships with other factors that are beyond the theory's scope. It is notable that in recent years few studies have addressed the push and pull theory at a theoretical level (Prayag & Ryan, 2011), and most research works are empirical studies applying the theory in different contexts.

The Travel Career Ladder and the Travel Career Pattern

Based on Maslow's (1959) motivation theory, Pearce and Caltabiano (1983) posited a "motivational career in travel" (p. 17), employing a fivefold classification of tourism motivation. This was later formally proposed as the *travel career ladder* (TCL; Pearce, 1988). This model considers that tourists gain experience from travel and this experience may lead to a hierarchical and developmental series of motivations, such that tourists have multiple motives for travel (Pearce, 1993). The TCL has received a number of criticisms. Witt and Wright (1992) considered that Maslow's motivation theory is not applicable to travel motivation, and a number of criticisms of the TCL were proposed by Ryan (1997, 1998): (a) the TCL is not a predictive theory and does not answer the question of why tourists move backwards and forwards on their career ladders (Ryan, 1998); (b) it cannot explain why some tourists pursue higher levels of need (i.e., self-esteem) without fulfilling lower ones (i.e., cleanliness; Ryan, 1997); (c) the number of items used to assess the ladder's levels is inadequate, which impacts the statistical and empirical validity of the approach (Pearce, 2005; Ryan, 1998); and (d) this model fails to recognize the importance of socialization while on holiday (Ryan, 1997).

Later, a modification of the TCL called the *travel career pattern* (TCP) was proposed by Pearce and Lee (2005). The TCP is a modification of the earlier TCL work that emphasizes the pattern of motivations and their structure rather than steps on a ladder or hierarchy. These researchers concluded that the patterns of motivations were related to *novelty*, *escape/relaxation*, *relationship*, and *self-development* regardless of one's tourism experience. Compared to the TCL, the TCP model reveals more meaningful information and explanations concerning tourists' motivations. The TCP is still under development as a tourist motivation model and more rigorous research is needed to test its validity (Hsu & Huang, 2008).

Functional Theory

The functional approach posits that the reason individuals hold certain attitudes is that these attitudes serve psychological needs. Embedding functional theory into the tourism motivation theory, people undertake leisure travel because the vacation serves (satisfies) an individual's psychological functions (needs; Fodness, 1994). Fodness (1994) developed an easy-to-administer self-report scale that relates leisure tourism to specific, generalizable motivators (Goossens, 2000), which provides a tool to explain the link between motivation and decision making, but it has been criticized for its lack of empirical rigor (Mansfeld, 1992), and further research is needed to determine its usefulness (Waller & Lea, 1998). Fodness (1994) also suggested that there needs to be more tests to explore its psychographic properties. Indeed, this model has not been widely used by other researchers perhaps because it is problematic to simply consider that the dimensions of previous research will be suitable for other populations (Huang & Hsu, 2005). In addition, some scholars considered that the functional theory will merely uncover many of the same sociological typologies advanced in the 1970s (Harrill & Potts, 2002).

Based on the above review of tourism motivation theory, the limitations identified are as follows: (a) the dimensions of motivation are not justified and are confusing or overlapping; (b) the motivation items used are at a relatively low psychology level such as attribute- and benefit-level motivation; (c) there is a lack of attention to relationships among the motivation dimensions. An alternative theory, MEC, is introduced here as a way to explore travel motivation and avoid these criticisms.

Means–End Chain Theory and Its Laddering Technique

The MEC theory is based on the expectancy–value theory (Gutman, 1997), which is widely used in marketing research to understand consumer behaviors. The MEC model seeks to explain how a product or service selection facilitates the achievement of desired end states (Gutman, 1982). MEC is an integrated approach to answering motivational questions with analytical rigor and theoretical sophistication. It is a straightforward method and provides actionable implications to researchers (Hawkins, Best, & Coney, 2004). Through MEC, there is a hierarchical ladder from the attributes that exist in products (the means), to the consequences (benefits) for the consumer provided by the attributes, to the personal values (the ends) the consequences reinforce (Gutman, 1982). For a finer-grained analysis of the mental representations regarding the product, each basic level of abstraction may be divided into two sublevels, leading to an MEC with six levels (Olson & Reynolds, 1983), ordered from low to high levels of abstraction (Figure 2).

Following in the tradition of MEC theory, the laddering technique is an associated research method developed by Reynolds and Gutman (1984). *Laddering* refers to an in-depth, one-on-one interviewing technique used to develop an understanding of how consumers translate the attributes of products into meaningful associations with respect

Figure 2. Six-level MEC model. Adapted from "The Means–End Approach to Understanding Consumer Decision-Making, by J. C. Olson and T. J. Reynolds, 2001, p. 14, in *Understanding Consumer Decision-Making: The Means–End Approach to Marketing and Advertising Strategy*, edited by T. J. Reynolds and J. C. Olson, Mahwah, NJ: Lawrence Erlbaum Associates.

to self (Reynolds & Gutman, 1988). The essence of this technique is that consumers are asked for concrete choice criteria they think are important when choosing a product (such as a vacation). Laddering assumes that choice elements can be sequentially elicited from the respondent to cause the respondent to think critically about the connections between the product's attributes and his or her personal motivation. With the typical interview question "Why is that important to you?" laddering enables hierarchical links to be investigated and recorded inductively among attribute, consequence, and value, thereby providing an understanding of motivation through an expression of outcomes at these three levels that are personally meaningful (McIntosh & Thyne, 2005).

In the field of tourism, the MEC theory is a useful approach for exploring psychological factors. The use of the MEC theory in tourism is not well developed and it has been suggested that this theory "has relevant and potential application in tourism research and, as such, should receive wider academic debate" (McIntosh & Thyne, 2005, p. 259). The MEC approach has been applied in studies such as destination choice (Klenosky & Gengler, 1993), accommodation choice (Mattila, 1999; Thyne & Lawson, 2001), museum and heritage visiting (Crotts & van Rekom, 1999; Jansen-Verbeke & van Rekom, 1996; McIntosh, 1999; Thyne, 2001), nature-based experiences (Frauman & Cunningham, 2001; Klenosky, Frauman, Norman, & Gengler, 1998), and the push and pull relationship (Klenosky, 2002). These studies enrich the literature on MEC theory in tourism research, but it is notable that the approach has not been widely used in motivation studies. In this article, a conceptual model is developed to explore Chinese outbound tourism motivations.

A Conceptual Model

There are two perspectives in MEC theory, motivational and cognitive. The conceptual model developed in this article (Figure 3) is based on the motivational perspective, which relies on values and value systems as the driving force for people's actions and is reflected in personalities, lifestyles, and motivations. In this view, attributes, consequences, and values all represent different motivational layers in an MEC analytic investigation of consumer motivation (Wagner, 2007). Therefore, this approach posits that motivation can be uncovered at different levels from low to high as underlying reasons why certain preferences are desired (Reynolds & Gutman, 1988).

Attributes represent aspects of the product or service and are physical or abstract in the way the product is perceived (Gutman, 1997). Motivation can be seen as the underlying reason why tourists choose a specific destination. Tourists tend to choose destinations that provide the attributes that most closely match their needs and expectations. Thus, destination attributes can be more motive specific and thus travel motives more clearly explain the reason underlying the preference for a destination. There are

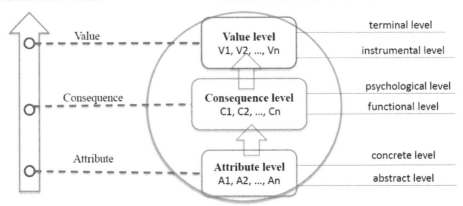

Figure 3. Conceptual model of Chinese outbound tourism motivation—an MEC approach (color figure avaialble online).

two types of attribute relevant to a tourism destination or product: a *concrete attribute* is an objective property of a tourism destination that attracts tourists, such as *local customs*, and an *abstract attribute* may be relative, instrumental, reflective, or vicarious, such as *famous* or *good environment*.

Consequences refers to any result (physiological or psychological) accruing directly or indirectly to the consumer from his or her behavior (Gutman, 1982). People choose certain behaviors for their expected results. Consequences can be categorized into functional and psychological/sociological types. *Functional consequence* refers to product features or attributes that produce immediate and tangible consequences (e.g., physiological needs) that are experienced directly by consumers. Functional consequences can lead to *psychological consequences*, which are more personal and affective or emotional (Olson & Reynolds, 2001), or *sociological* consequences (Gutman, 1982). In tourism motivation, "improved personal relationships" or "to enrich one's knowledge" can be regarded as functional consequences, whereas "to satisfy one's curiosity" is a psychological consequence.

Values are defined as "learned beliefs that serve as guiding principles about how individuals ought to behave" (Parks & Guay, 2009, p. 676). Similarly, values are "an enduring belief that a specific mode of conduct or end-state of existence is personally or socially preferable to an opposite or converse mode of conduct or end-state of existence" (Rokeach, 1973, p. 5). The primary content of a value is the type of goal or motivational concern that it expresses (Schwartz & Bilsky, 1987), and values have been shown to be a powerful force in governing the behaviors of individuals in all aspects of their lives (Gutman, 1982). Thus, it is necessary to explore tourism motivation through deep enquiry at the value level. There are two kinds of values: *instrumental* values are related to a mode of conduct, and a *terminal* value is the end-state of existence. In tourism, for example, one of the motivations to travel may be "knowledge seeking" at an instrumental value level or the motivation of an "exciting life" at a terminal value level.

Using the terms explained above, this conceptual framework is intended to serve three purposes: prescriptively, it guides the conceptualization and process of tourism motivation; analytically, it facilitates the critical examination and hierarchical categorization of tourism motivation levels and items; and methodologically, it points to criteria and a precautionary standard that the research should apply in exploring motivation during data collection.

This conceptual model is considered to provide a directed, hierarchically organized structure of interconnected levels of tourism motivation. Attributes of a tourism destination are perceived by tourists as a means to obtain desired consequences that in turn lead to the achievement of values. By avoiding mixing the dimension of motivation during application and analysis, the above model not only explores the motivations within their different levels but examines the internal relationships of motivation behind each level to better understand travel motivation as a whole.

In summary, the MEC theory introduced in this study provides a way to understand why Chinese people make decisions on outbound travel and the reasons why they choose a specific tourism destination. These reasons can be identified as travel motivations at different levels of the MEC, and they also explain how these motivation facets at different levels are salient or self-relevant to tourists. In this sense, then, this MEC framework not only describes but also explains travel motivation.

Proposed Laddering Interview Process

Laddering is a related technique for data collection based on the MEC theory. There are two approaches in the laddering technique—hard laddering and soft laddering. *Soft laddering* is more frequently used in discursive interviews and is an inductive analysis technique to uncover ladders, because the respondents' natural flow of speech is restricted as little as possible (McDonald, Thyne, & McMorland, 2008). As a result, soft laddering is useful when respondents cannot or will not express their end values/goals; the researcher diagnoses the end value from the transcripts (McDonald et al., 2008).

To conduct a laddering interview, a relaxing interview environment has to be created for respondents so that they feel comfortable and are willing to tell their true feelings and look inside themselves for the underlying motivations. For example, the interview can begin with a general introduction mentioning the main purpose of the research, followed by general questions regarding previous outbound tourism experiences. After this warm-up phase, the discussion then focuses on the respondent's next destination for outbound leisure travel and the main reasons (attributes) for choosing this destination. The respondent is encouraged to list between four and seven key attributes used for choosing the destination. After the respondent has described all of the key attributes, the researcher can ask him or her questions using the laddering procedure "Why is that important to you?" This laddering question will be asked until the respondent cannot give more answers or it reaches the value-level motivations. It is critical that this technique be applied to each attribute identified to obtain the motivations at the attribute, consequence, and value levels.

Implications

It is believed that the use of MEC theory will provide useful insights for better understanding of tourism motivations and the behavioral characteristics of Chinese outbound leisure tourists. Specifically, the above model provides the following implications. First, the conceptual model provides a directed, hierarchically organized structure with interconnected levels to explain how a product or service selection facilitates the achievement of desired end states. In previous studies of tourism motivation, not all tourists' motivations can be identified from the tourists directly due to the subjects' uncertainty about their travel needs, and "in many cases, when the subjects were asked to describe the reasons for travelling to the particular country, they simply provided their image of the destination from their memory rather than expressing themselves with motivational statements" (Pearce & Lee, 2005, p. 229). Respondents' lack of awareness of their travel motives can be classified under four headings: tourists may not wish to reflect on real travel motives, may be unable to reflect on real travel motives, may not wish to express real travel motives, or may not be able to express real travel motives (Dann, 1981). The conceptual framework in this article represents a new approach in exploring the leisure tourism motivation of Chinese outbound tourists by identifying the reasons behind tourism motivation not only at different levels of the MEC but also in explaining how these motivation facets of different levels are salient or self-relevant to tourists. In this way, the MEC approach is believed to contribute to the body of knowledge on motivation studies by better understanding respondents' motives and the underlying needs or motives being sought (Jewell & Crotts, 2001).

Second, at the methodological level, on the one hand, the model provides dimensions and levels for motivation measurement. It allows discovery of the key descriptors at all levels, as well as their connection and linkages, which provide the structural components of tourism motivation (Crotts & van Rekom, 1999). The laddering technique is superior in that it allows respondents to think about their underlying motivations distinct from their surface reasons. Determining the attribute, benefit, and value levels of tourism motivation can help us better understand tourism motivation and provide useful information on tourism behaviors (Klenosky, 2002).

Third, the need to understand personal values in tourism motivations has been noted (Kim & Prideaux, 2005), and it has been suggested that tourism motivation theory should consider the long-term goals, and it is not a simple short-term process (Pearce, 1982; Uysal & Hagan, 1993). As a tourism motivation theory, important issues such as long-term goals, the perspective of the observer, multi-motive causes of behavior, measurement issues, and the qualitative nature of intrinsically motivated behaviors should be considered (Pearce & Stringer, 1991). It is believed that MEC theory provides a useful way to investigate tourism motivations at the value level that allows for long-term behavioral patterns to be better understood.

Fourth, this model provides a basis for understanding more specific reasons why Chinese tourists make decisions on outbound tourism and why they choose a specific tourism destination. According to Pearce (2005), much work on tourism motivation has used U.S.-based samples and problems may be posed in the universality of findings when constructing theories that apply across cultures (Smith, 1995). As an Eastern society, Chinese tourists have their unique culture and values and, therefore, conceptualizations and meanings of leisure tourism derived from U.S. studies do not necessarily apply in China, because "there may be specific factors unique to the Chinese culture, language and also expectation" (Junek, Binney, & Deery, 2004, p. 150). Although MEC theory has been applied in various tourism research studies, there is as yet no research applying this theory on Chinese outbound tourists. This approach could contribute to the literature on developing and confirming suitable theories and methodologies in the motivation research on Chinese outbound tourists.

Conclusion and Future Study

Due to the need for pluralism in perspective in tourism and its multidisciplinary nature (Dann, 1981), this research suggests the application of MEC theory to the study of tourism motivation. It is concluded that MEC theory has a number of significant advantages in understanding tourism motivation. Theoretically, the MEC approach allows exploration of tourism motivation by determining the attributes, consequences, and values that motivate tourism behavior within hierarchical levels and the relationships between each level, which can clearly identify the dimensions and levels of motivation; methodologically, it can lead respondents to think about their underlying motivations better and could provide insights for tourism motivation research in terms of the connection between personal values and tourism attributes. It is argued that exploring tourism motivation with MEC will make both theoretical and methodological contributions to tourism research, as well as provide more meaningful information for understanding Chinese outbound tourists as an emerging market.

Limitations of the MEC research are that much prior MEC research is proprietary and has been conducted for consulting purposes to address practical marketing problems, suggesting that further study is needed to develop MEC theory as a complete and formalized theory. As a little-used approach in tourism motivation research, more empirical work to support this theory is required, especially in the context of various cultural backgrounds. Another challenge is that laddering requires relatively highly skilled interview techniques. For example, during an interview, the more respondents move up the levels of abstraction, the more they may feel difficult and discomfort with the "why" questions. This may be because values are personal in nature (Veludo-de-Oliveira, Ikeda, & Campomar, 2006). Therefore, time and practice are necessary to conduct such research.

References

Braun, O. L. (1989). *Vom alltagsstress zur urlaubszufriedenheit* [From daily stress to holiday satisfaction] (Unpublished doctoral dissertation). University of Bielefeld, Belfield, Germany.

Chen, Y., Mak, B., & McKercher, B. (2011). What drives people to travel: Integrating the tourist motivation paradigms. *Journal of China Tourism Research, 7*(2), 120–136.

China National Tourism Administration. (n.d.). *China tourism industry statistics bulletin.* Retrieved from http://www.cnta.gov.cn/html/zh/index.html

China Tourism Association. (2010). *The report from the Sixth China Outbound Tourism Forum.* Beijing, China: Author.

Chul Oh, H., Uysal, M., & Weaver, P. (1995). Product bundles and market segments based on travel motivations: A canonical correlation approach. *International Journal of Hospitality Management, 14*(2), 123–137.

Crompton, J. L. (1979). Motivations for pleasure vacation. *Annals of Tourism Research, 6*(4), 408–424.

Crotts, J., & van Rekom, J. (1999). Exploring and enhancing the psychological value of a fine arts museum. *Journal of International Hospitality, Leisure & Tourism Management, 1*(4), 37–48.

Dann, G. (1977). Anomie, ego-enhancement and tourism. *Annals of Tourism Research, 4*(4), 184–194.

Dann, G. (1981). Tourist motivation: An appraisal. *Annals of Tourism Research, 8*(2), 187–219.

Dann, G., Nash, D., & Pearce, P. (1988). Methodology in tourism research. *Annals of Tourism Research, 15*(1), 1–28.

Dunn Ross, E. L., & Iso-Ahola, S. E. (1991). Sightseeing tourists' motivation and satisfaction. *Annals of Tourism Research, 18*(2), 226–237.

Fodness, D. (1994). Measuring tourist motivation. *Annals of Tourism Research*, *21*(3), 555–581.

Frauman, E., & Cunningham, P. (2001). Using a means–end approach to understand the factors that influence greenway use. *Journal of Park and Recreation Administration*, *19*(3), 93–113.

Gnoth, J. (1997). Tourism motivation and expectation formation. *Annals of Tourism Research*, *24*(2), 283–304.

Goossens, C. (2000). Tourism information and pleasure motivation. *Annals of Tourism Research*, *27*(2), 301–321.

Gutman, J. (1982). A means–end chain model based on consumer categorization processes. *Journal of Marketing*, *46*(2), 60–72.

Gutman, J. (1997). Means–end chains as goal hierarchies. *Psychology and Marketing*, *14*(6), 545–560.

Harrill, R., & Potts, T. D. (2002). Social psychological theories of tourist motivation: Exploration, debate and transition. *Tourism Analysis*, *7*(2), 105–114.

Hawkins, D. I., Best, R. J., & Coney, K. A. (2004). *Consumer behavior: Building marketing strategy*. Boston, MA: McGraw-Hill Irwin.

Hsu, C. H. C., & Huang, S. (2008). Travel motivation: A critical review of the concept's development. In A. G. Woodside & D. Martin (Eds.), *Tourism management: Analysis, behaviour and strategy* (pp. 14–27). Oxfordshire, England: CAB International.

Huang, S., & Hsu, C. H. C. (2005). Mainland Chinese residents' perceptions and motivations of visiting Hong Kong: Evidence from focus group interviews. *Asia Pacific Journal of Tourism Research*, *10*(2), 191–205.

Iso-Ahola, S. E. (1982). Toward a social psychological theory of tourism motivation: A rejoinder. *Annals of Tourism Research*, *9*(2), 256–262.

Jafari, J. (1987). Tourism models: The socio-cultural aspects. *Tourism Management*, *8*(2), 151–159.

Jamal, T., & Lee, J.-H. (2003). Integrating micro and macro approaches to tourist motivations: Toward an interdisciplinary theory. *Tourism Analysis*, *8*(1), 47–59.

Jang, S., & Wu, C.-M. E. (2006). Seniors' travel motivation and the influential factors: An examination of Taiwanese seniors. *Tourism Management*, *27*(2), 306–316.

Jansen-Verbeke, M., & van Rekom, J. (1996). Scanning museum visitors: Urban tourism marketing. *Annals of Tourism Research*, *23*(2), 364–375.

Jewell, B., & Crotts, J. C. (2001). Adding psychological value to heritage tourism experiences. *Journal of Travel & Tourism Marketing*, *11*(4), 13–28.

Junek, O., Binney, W., & Deery, M. (2004). Meeting the needs of the Chinese tourist: The operators' perspective. *ASEAN Journal on Hospitality and Tourism*, *3*(2), 149–161.

Kim, S. S., & Lee, C.-K. (2002). Push and pull relationships. *Annals of Tourism Research*, *29*(1), 257–260.

Kim, S. S., & Prideaux, B. (2005). Marketing implications arising from a comparative study of international pleasure tourist motivations and other travel-related characteristics of visitors to Korea. *Tourism Management*, *26*(3), 347–357.

Klenosky, D. B. (2002). The "pull" of tourism destinations: A means–end investigation. *Journal of Travel Research*, *40*(4), 385–395.

Klenosky, D. B., Frauman, E., Norman, W., & Gengler, C. (1998). Nature-based tourists' use of interpretive services: A means–end investigation. *Journal of Tourism Studies*, *9*(2), 26–36.

Klenosky, D. B., & Gengler, C. E. (1993). Understanding the factors influencing ski destination choice: A means–end analytic approach. *Journal of Leisure Research*, *25*(4), 362–379.

Kluin, J. Y., & Lehto, X. Y. (2012). Measuring family reunion travel motivations. *Annals of Tourism Research*, *39*(2), 820–841.

Kozak, M. (2002). Comparative analysis of tourist motivations by nationality and destinations. *Tourism Management*, *23*(3), 221–232.

Mannell, R. C., & Iso-Ahola, S. E. (1987). Psychological nature of leisure and tourism experience. *Annals of Tourism Research*, *14*(3), 314–331.

Mansfeld, Y. (1992). From motivation to actual travel. *Annals of Tourism Research, 19*(3), 399–419.

Maslow, A. H. (1959). *Motivaiton and personality*. New York, NY: Harper and Row.

Mattila, A. (1999). An analysis of means–end hierarchies in cross-cultural context: What motivates Asian and Western business travellers to stay at luxury hotels? *Journal of Hospitality & Leisure Marketing, 6*(2), 19–28.

McDonald, S., Thyne, M., & McMorland, L.-A. (2008). Means–end theory in tourism research. *Annals of Tourism Research, 35*(2), 596–599.

McIntosh, A. J. (1999). Affirming authenticity: Consuming cultural heritage. *Annals of Tourism Research, 26*(3), 589–612.

McIntosh, A. J., & Thyne, M. A. (2005). Understanding tourist behavior using means–end chain theory. *Annals of Tourism Research, 32*(1), 259–262.

McKercher, B. (2005). Are psychographics predictors of destination life cycles? *Journal of Travel & Tourism Marketing, 19*(1), 49–55.

National Bureau of Statistics of China. (n.d.). 2011 Gross domestic product (GDP). Retrieved from http://www.stats.gov.cn/tjsj/jdsj/t20120118_402779799.htm

Olson, J. C., & Reynolds, T. J. (1983). Understanding consumers' cognitive structures: Implications for advertising strategy. In L. Percy & A. G. Woodside (Eds.), *Advertising and consumer psychology* (pp. 77–90). Lexington, MA: Lexington Books.

Olson, J. C., & Reynolds, T. J. (2001). The means–end approach to understanding consumer decision-making. In T. J. Reynolds & J. C. Olson (Eds.), *Understanding consumer decision-making: The means–end approach to marketing and advertising strategy* (pp. 3–20). Mahwah, NJ: Lawrence Erlbaum Associates.

Parks, L., & Guay, R. P. (2009). Personality, values, and motivation. *Personality and Individual Differences, 47*(7), 675–684.

Pearce, P. (1982). *The social psychology of tourist behavior*. Oxford, UK: New Pergamon Press.

Pearce, P. (1988). *The Ulysses factor: Evaluating visitors in tourist settings*. New York, NY: Springer-Verlag.

Pearce, P. (1993). Fundamentals of tourist motivation. In D. G. Pearce & R. W. Butler (Eds.), *Tourism research: Critiques and challenges* (pp. 113–134). New York, NY: Routledge.

Pearce, P. (2005). *Tourist behaviour: Themes and conceptual schemes*. Clevedon, England: Channel View Publications.

Pearce, P., & Caltabiano, M. L. (1983). Inferring travel motivation from travelers' experiences. *Journal of Travel Research, 22*(2), 16–20.

Pearce, P., & Lee, U.-I. (2005). Developing the travel career approach to tourist motivation. *Journal of Travel Research, 43*(3), 226–237.

Pearce, P., & Stringer, P. F. (1991). Psychology and tourism. *Annals of Tourism Research, 18*(1), 136–154.

Petri, H., & Govern, J. (2004). *Motivation: Theory, research, and applications /* (5th ed.). Belmont, CA: Wadsworth Publishing Company.

Plog, S. C. (1974). Why destination areas rise and fall in popularity. *Cornell Hotel and Restaurant Administration Quarterly, 16*(1), 55–58.

Plog, S. C. (2001). Why destination areas rise and fall in popularity: An update of a Cornell Quarterly classic. *Cornell Hotel and Restaurant Administration Quarterly, 42*(3), 13–24.

Plog, S. C. (2002). The power of psychographics and the concept of venturesomeness. *Journal of Travel Research, 40*(3), 244–251.

Prayag, G., & Ryan, C. (2011). The relationship between the "push" and "pull" factors of a tourist destination: The role of nationality—An analytical qualitative research approach. *Current Issues in Tourism, 14*(2), 121–143.

Reynolds, T. J., & Gutman, J. (1984). Advertising is image management. *Journal of Advertising Research, 24*(1), 27–37.

Reynolds, T. J., & Gutman, J. (1988). Laddering theory, method, analysis, and interpretation. *Journal of Advertising Research, 28*(1), 11–31.

Rokeach, M. (1973). *The nature of human values*. New York, NY: The Free Press.

Ryan, C. (1997). *The tourist experience*. London, England: Cassell.

Ryan, C. (1998). The travel career ladder: An appraisal. *Annals of Tourism Research, 25*(4), 936–957.

Schwartz, S. H., & Bilsky, W. (1987). Toward a psychological structure and cotents of human values. *Journal of Personality and Social Psychology, 53*, 550–562.

Shao, Q. (2012). The speech on 2011 national tourism work conference. Retrieved from http://www.cnta.gov.cn/html/2012-1/2012-1-16-9-23-93087.html

Smith, S. (1995). *Tourism analysis: A handbook*. Harlow, England: Longman.

Snepenger, D., King, J., Marshall, E., & Uysal, M. (2006). Modeling Iso-Ahola's motivation theory in the tourism context. *Journal of Travel Research, 45*(2), 140–149.

Thyne, M. (2001). The importance of values research for nonprofit organisations: The motivation-based values of museum visitors. *International Journal of Nonprofit and Voluntary Sector Marketing, 6*(2), 116–130.

Thyne, M., & Lawson, R. (2001). Values as a basis for understanding motivations towards accommodation and activity choices. In M. Robinson, P. Long, N. Evans, R. Sharpley, & J. Swarbrooke (Eds.), *Reflections on international tourism: Motivations, behaviour and tourist types* (pp. 431–454). Sunderland, England: Centre for Tourism in association with Business Education Publishers.

Tse, T. S. M., & Hobson, J. S. P. (2008). The forces shaping China's outbound tourism. *Journal of China Tourism Research, 4*(2), 136–155.

Uysal, M., & Hagan, L. (1993). Motivation of pleasure travel and tourism. In M. A. Khan, M. D. Olsen, & T. Var (Eds.), *VNR's encyclopedia of hospitality and tourism* (pp. 798–810). New York, NY: Van Nostrand Reinhold.

Uysal, M., & Jurowski, C. (1994). Testing the push and pull factors. *Annals of Tourism Research, 21*(4), 844–846.

Veludo-de-Oliveira, T. M., Ikeda, A. A., & Campomar, M. C. (2006). Laddering in the practice of marketing research: Barriers and solutions. *Qualitative Market Research, 9*(3), 297–306.

Wagner, T. (2007). Shopping motivation revised: A means–end chain analytical perspective. *International Journal of Retail & Distribution Management, 35*(7), 569–582.

Waller, J., & Lea, E. G. S. (1998). Seeking the real Spain? Authenticity in motivation. *Annals of Tourism Research, 26*(1), 110–129.

White, C. J., & Thompson, M. (2009). Self determination theory and the wine club attribute formation process. *Annals of Tourism Research, 36*(4), 561–586.

Witt, C. A., & Wright, P. L. (1992). Tourist motivation: Life after Maslow. In B. Thomas & P. S. Johnson (Eds.), *Choice and demand in tourism* (pp. 33–55). London, England: Mansell.

World Tourism Organization. (2003). *Chinese outbound tourism*. Madrid, Spain.

Yuan, S., & McDonald, C. (1990). Motivational determinates of international pleasure time. *Journal of Travel Research, 29*(1), 42–44.

Comparing Mainland Chinese Tourists' Satisfaction With Hong Kong and the UK Using Tourist Satisfaction Index

基于旅客满意指数比较中国大陆旅客对香港和英国的满意度

GANG LI
HAIYAN SONG
JASON LI CHEN
DORIS CHENGUANG WU

This study aims to assess Mainland Chinese tourists' satisfaction with the UK and Hong Kong using a Tourist Satisfaction Index (TSI) approach. Based on a survey with Mainland Chinese tourists in the UK who also visited Hong Kong recently, this study computes the overall destination TSIs and sectoral TSIs for both Hong Kong and the UK. The results suggest that, overall, Mainland Chinese tourists were more satisfied with Hong Kong than with the UK as their travel destination. With respect to individual service sectors, Mainland Chinese tourists were more satisfied with six out of the seven surveyed tourism-related service sectors in Hong Kong than their counterparts in the UK. Visitor attractions, hotels, and local tour operators show the most significant contribution to Mainland Chinese tourists' overall satisfaction evaluation in both destinations. These findings suggest that Hong Kong's tourism industry as a whole is more competitive than that of the UK as far as Mainland Chinese tourists are concerned. Cross-cultural perspectives should be adopted in tourism service operations at an international tourist destination.

本研究采用旅客满意指数(TSI)方法，旨在评估中国大陆旅客对英国和香港的满意度。基于对最近曾到访香港、现正身处英国的中国大陆旅客的调查，本研究对香港和英国两地的整体目的地满意指数和不同行业的满意指数进行了计算和评估。结果显示，中国大陆旅客对香港作为旅游目的地的满意度整体高于英国。从七个旅游相关服务行业的比较结果来看，在其中六个行业中，中国大陆旅客对香港的满意度均高于英国。旅游景点、酒店及当地旅行社是影响中国旅客对香港和英国两地的整体满意评价的三个主要因素。本文研究结果指出，就中国

Gang Li is a Reader in Tourism Economics in the School of Hospitality and Tourism Management at the University of Surrey, Guildford, UK.

Haiyan Song is a Chair Professor of Tourism in the School of Hotel and Tourism Management at The Hong Kong Polytechnic University, Kowloon, Hong Kong, China.

Jason Li Chen is a Lecturer in Tourism and Events Management in the School of Hospitality and Tourism Management at the University of Surrey, Guildford, UK.

Doris Chenguang Wu is an Assistant Professor in the SunYat-sen Business School at Sun Yat-sen University, Guangzhou, China.

大陆旅客而言，香港旅游业整体上较英国更具竞争力。在国际旅游目的地的旅游服务运营方面应采用跨文化观点。

关键词：旅客满意指数，中国旅客，结构方程模型，香港，英国

Introduction

Rapid economic development in China has led to a dramatic increase in personal disposable income, an improved standard of living, and a burgeoning Chinese middle class with enormous spending power and the desire to travel abroad. The number of Mainland Chinese outbound tourists increased from 3.74 million in 1993 to 57.4 million in 2010, representing an annual growth of 17.4% on average (United Nations World Tourism Organization [UNWTO], 2003; Zhang, Song, & Liu, 2011). Despite the global economic downturn, the number of outbound trips by Chinese tourists still increased by 21% in 2010 (Zhang et al., 2011). In addition, their expenditure during outbound travel increased by 17% in the same year against the previous one (Zhang et al., 2011). A substantial increase in Mainland Chinese outbound tourists was noted in the World Tourism Organization Tourism Vision 2020 report, which forecasts 100 million Mainland Chinese outbound tourists by 2020 (UNWTO, 1999). This number will account for 6.2% of the world's outbound tourist market and ranks fourth among outbound tourist generating countries, following German, Japanese, and U.S. tourists (UNWTO, 1999).

The significant contribution of Chinese outbound tourism to world tourism development has been recognized by many tourist destinations, and strategic plans have been developed to target and compete for this emerging market. Therefore, it is important for the tourism industry in these destinations to understand the behavior of this market and provide satisfactory services to meet their needs and wants in order to gain and maintain competitiveness. Although increasing attention has been paid to this rising market, more in-depth, vigorous marketing research is still needed (Chon, 2005; Wang & Davidson, 2010). The present study aims to bring a new addition to the literature.

Tourist satisfaction has become an increasingly important issue for many destinations and tourism sectors that rely primarily on inbound tourists, such as Hong Kong. Satisfied tourists are more likely to recommend the destination to their friends and relatives. This is the most effective way to promote a tourist destination. In addition, tourist satisfaction could contribute to the increased rates of retention of tourists' patronage, loyalty, and acquisition (Li & Carr, 2004), which will have an important impact on the destination's economic growth in general.

The current study extends the research on Chinese outbound tourists' behaviors with particular attention paid to Chinese tourists' satisfaction with their various tourism experiences in a comparative setting. Two popular destinations for Chinese outbound travel were selected for comparison in this study: Hong Kong and the UK. Hong Kong is the top destination of Chinese outbound tourism and received 22.7 million Chinese visitors in 2010, which accounts for 40% of total outbound visits from China. This number also represents 63% of total inbound visitor arrivals in Hong Kong in 2010 (Hong Kong Tourism Board, 2011; Zhang et al., 2011). Therefore, the importance of the Mainland Chinese market for the Hong Kong tourism industry is well understood. Britain is a fast-growing long-haul destination for Chinese outbound tourism. In addition to the geographical distance, there is a great cultural distance between China and the UK, which is a key pull factor that attracts Chinese tourists to the UK. The UK received 109,000 visitors from China and attracted 184 million pounds in tourism spending from this market in 2010 (VisitBritain, 2012). Although the UK's market share of Chinese outbound tourism is still low, its growth has been significant. The number of Chinese tourist arrivals and their spending increased by 15% and 40% respectively between 2005 and 2010 (VisitBritain, 2012). According to VisitBritain's forecasts, visits from China to the UK are expected to grow at a faster rate (89%) than from any other source market by 2014, bringing just under 100,000 more tourists to the country (VisitBritain, 2010a). According to VisitBritain's research, increasing the UK's share of the Chinese outbound tourism market by half a percent would generate an additional 2.5 billion pounds for the economy and create 50,000 new jobs (VisitBritain, 2010b). Given the great economic contribution of this market to the UK economy, especially under the current economic climate, it is important to understand the behavioral characteristics of this market and to enhance their satisfaction with the travel experience in the UK.

This study aims to evaluate Mainland Chinese tourists' satisfaction with Hong Kong in comparison to their satisfaction with the UK. The contrasts between the two selected destinations allow an in-depth analysis leading to an enhanced understanding of Chinese tourists' behavioral characteristics. This is an extension of the studies by Song, Li, van der Veen, and Chen (2011) and Song, van der Veen, Li, and Chen (2012), who developed a Tourist Satisfaction Index (TSI) framework. This comparative study aims to achieve the following objectives:

1. To evaluate Mainland Chinese tourists' satisfaction with key tourism-related service sectors in Hong Kong and in the UK.
2. To assess Mainland Chinese tourists' overall satisfaction with Hong Kong and the UK based on the developed TSI conceptual model.
3. To investigate the relationships between sectoral satisfaction and overall satisfaction in Hong Kong and in the UK.
4. To compute the sectoral and overall tourist satisfaction indexes for Hong Kong and the UK.
5. To compare Mainland Chinese tourists' satisfaction with Hong Kong and the UK based on the computed satisfaction indexes.

By achieving the above objectives, the applicability of the developed TSI framework will be further verified. Moreover, new empirical evidence will be provided with regard to destination competitiveness in relation to Chinese outbound tourism. Useful implications can be drawn for the related tourism businesses and destination management organizations in these destinations.

Literature Review

Consumer satisfaction (CS) has always been one of the most important issues addressed by marketers, because a good understanding of CS is imperative for a firm to establish a long-term relationship with customers and to maintain long-term competitiveness (Henning-Thurau & Klee, 1997). CS has been exhaustively researched over the last few decades. Although various approaches to the measurement of CS have been developed, a consensus has not yet been reached. Among various CS theories, three satisfaction models have attracted the most attention in the literature: the expectation–perception paradigm (Parasuraman, Zeithaml, & Berry, 1985), the performance-only model (Grönroos, 1984), and the expectancy–disconfirmation model (Oliver, 1980).

The expectation–perception paradigm considers CS to be a reflection of either positive or negative gaps between the initial consumer expectations and perceptions of a product's performance, whereas the performance-only model regards CS as "an outcome of the actual quality of performance and its perception by consumers" (Kozak & Rimmington, 2000, p. 261). The shortcoming of the performance-only model is that "it is impossible to interpret high levels of customer satisfaction as the results of low expectations or superior quality of service provider" (Fuchs & Weiermair, 2004, p. 215). The expectation–perception approach is also criticized because consumers' expectations may be updated once they receive further information about the goods or services (Boulding, Kalra, Staeling, & Zeithaml, 1993; Kozak & Rimmington, 2000). The expectancy–disconfirmation model is further developed based on the expectation–perception concept. According to the theory, a customer has established certain expectations of the performance of the goods or services before purchasing them, and he or she tends to make comparison between the actual performance of the goods or services and his or her anticipation after consumption. Disconfirmation thus arises from the comparison. If the actual performance of the goods/services surpasses the expectation, positive disconfirmation is reached, which would then lead to the consumer's satisfaction and willingness to repurchase. If the actual performance fails to meet the initial expectation, negative disconfirmation arrives. Within the expectancy–disconfirmation framework, a number of other models have been applied to CS studies, such as the congruity model (Sirgy, 1984), which suggests that CS depends on a comparison of the perceived performance of the goods or services concerned relative to the hypothetical ideal performance that a consumer can imagine. The more congruence between the perceived and ideal performance, the more satisfied a consumer is likely to be. Other CS theories that have been developed include equity, attribution, comparison level, generalized negativity, value-precept, and so on (Oh & Parks, 1997).

In the tourism literature, most of the above approaches have been applied to examine tourist satisfaction (TS) in various empirical contexts. Some studies focused on the overall levels of TS with a destination (e.g., Kau & Lim, 2005), whereas others paid attention to specific attributes at the service encounter level, such as a hotel, restaurant, travel agent, attraction, transport service, and retail shop (e.g., Heung, 2000; Wang, Vela, & Tyler, 2008). The expectation–disconfirmation paradigm has become the most commonly applied theoretical foundation in TS research, given its broadly applicable conceptualization. In addition to the importance for tourism service providers, the direct relevance of TS to destination competitiveness is well noted (Wong & Law, 2003).

With regard to the measurement of TS, most studies use traditional single-item scales to obtain tourists' responses ranging from *very dissatisfied* to *very satisfied*. The drawbacks of this approach have been noted in the general CS literature, such as failure to capture the complexity of satisfaction evaluation and greater possibility of measurement errors in a survey (Chan et al., 2003; Yi, 1990). As a result, the reliability of the findings is challenged (Yi, 1990). More recent satisfaction research regarded satisfaction as a theoretical construct or latent variable that cannot be measured directly. Therefore, multi-item scales are more desirable to measure satisfaction. In an empirical study, Oliver (1980) showed that multi-item scales are significantly more reliable than single-item scales. In the tourism literature, most TS studies still employ single-item scales to measure the overall satisfaction, with few exceptions, such as Yoon and Uysal (2005). In this study, four indicators are developed (and three are finally used) based on the expectancy–disconfirmation model, the performance-only model, the equality theory, and the norm theory, respectively. Future TS studies should consider such multi-item measurement.

Although tourist satisfaction has been extensively studied in the past few decades, only a few studies have explored the issue in the context of Chinese outbound tourism. Focusing on Australia as a destination for Chinese outbound travel, Li and Carr (2004) found that Chinese tourists were more satisfied with natural attractions and a clean and safe environment but less satisfied with shopping, food, and prices in Australia. Ryan and Mo (2001) found that Chinese tourists were also satisfied with cultural attractions in New Zealand. Based on the service quality framework "SERVQUAL," Wang et al. (2008) found that Chinese tourists were dissatisfied with all 33 hotel attributes, including restaurant services, in the hotels in the UK. Communication barriers and different food cultures were identified as key issues. Kau and Lim (2005) examined the level of satisfaction of Chinese tourists in Singapore and segmented the sample according to tourists' travel motivations. They found that the overall satisfaction level of family/relaxation seekers was significantly higher than that of prestige/knowledge seekers, adventure/pleasure seekers, and novelty seekers, with the last group being least satisfied. A few studies have focused on Chinese tourists' satisfaction with tourism services and facilities in Hong Kong. For instance, Qu and Li (1997) found that Chinese tourists were satisfied with the infrastructure and facilities, environment, and tourism services but dissatisfied with prices for shopping and accommodation in Hong Kong. Using the disconfirmation model, Heung (2000) found that Chinese tourists were dissatisfied with 20 out of 34 Hong Kong hotel attributes. Chinese tourists were generally less satisfied with the accommodations than other services when traveling abroad. All of these studies focused on a single international destination. So far, no comparative study has been found regarding Chinese tourists' satisfaction with different destinations. Thus, the potential difference in Chinese tourists' travel behaviors and experiences at different destinations, especially those with great cultural distance, is not well understood. In addition, a comparison of destination competitiveness concerning the Chinese tourist market is not possible without such a comparative setting. The present study aims to bridge this gap in the literature.

The interest in CS assessment has driven scholars and practitioners to further develop consumer satisfaction indexes (CSIs) to monitor the changes in household satisfaction with goods and services purchased over time. However, no attempt has been made to comprehensively and continuously assess CS in the tourism context until the development of the Hong Kong TSI (Song et al., 2011, 2012). The Hong Kong TSI framework is based on the previously developed CSIs, especially the Hong Kong CSI model (Chan et al., 2003), but has its own unique features. First of all, the Hong Kong TSI is a two-stage tourist satisfaction evaluation system starting with a sectoral-level assessment, which is then aggregated to the overall destination level. Secondly, aggregation of the sectoral TSIs for computing the overall TSI is based on an innovative weighting scheme that is determined by the tourists' own evaluations. As a result, free-of-charge and other public services can be included in compilation of the TSI. Thirdly, TSIs at both the sectoral and destination levels can be estimated and their relationships can be examined directly; therefore, more useful policy implications can be derived for effective destination management. Figure 1 shows a conceptual model of tourist satisfaction assessment, in which *tourist characteristics*, *expectations*, *perceived performance*, and *assessed value* are antecedents of *tourist satisfaction*, and *tourist complaints* and *loyalty* are consequences of *tourist satisfaction*. Each sectoral TSI is computed

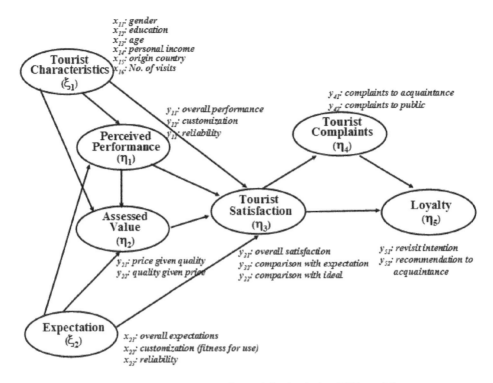

Figure 1. Hong Kong tourist satisfaction index (TSI) model.

based on this model. All sectoral TSIs are further aggregated to the overall destination TSI using confirmatory factor analysis.

The above developed Hong Kong TSI framework was empirically tested based on a pilot study on Mainland Chinese tourists' satisfaction with three selected service sectors, including hotels, retail shops, and local tour operators in Hong Kong. The computed sectoral TSIs were 76.78, 73.01, and 72.82 out of 100, respectively. The aggregated overall TSI was 74.04, with the retail sector contributing the most to Chinese tourists' overall satisfaction, followed by the hotel sector and the local tour operator sector (Song et al., 2011). The *tourist characteristics* construct did not have a significant influence on *assessed value*, *perceived performance*, or *tourist satisfaction* and was therefore removed from the final sectoral TSI model. Similar results were reached in the subsequent main study (Song et al., 2012), which covered all major source markets and six key tourism sectors, including attractions, hotels, immigration services, restaurants, retail shops, and transportation. Based on the above Hong Kong TSI framework and the research instrument developed, the current study aims to further verify the theoretical model in a new and comparative setting.

Methodology

This study adopts the general TSI framework developed by Song et al. (2011, 2012). Different from previous research designs, this study applies the theoretical model of TSI in Figure 1 to the overall destination satisfaction assessment instead of the evaluation of each of the key tourism-related sectors. This research design is more suitable for a comparative study because the original design would double the length of the survey and thus data collection would be extremely difficult. In the current study, sectoral-level tourist satisfaction is also examined in order to establish the relationship with the overall satisfaction, but the antecedents and consequences of sectoral-level satisfaction are beyond the scope of this comparative study and hence were excluded from the survey. The research instrument was developed based on studies by Song et al. (2011, 2012). The survey consisted of four parts: overall destination satisfaction assessment of the UK, overall destination satisfaction assessment of Hong Kong, sectoral-level satisfaction assessment of both the UK and Hong Kong, and demographics. In Parts 1 and 2, all constructs of the theoretical model in Figure 1 were included, measured by multiple items (see Figure 1). It should be noted that the tourist characteristics construct did not present any significant relationships with other constructs in the previous two studies; this study attempts to verify the finding by introducing the construct in the initial modeling process and examining the statistical significance of the relevant path coefficients. If none of the path coefficients is statistically significant, this construct will be dropped from the model. An 11-point rating scale from 0 for *poor* to 10 for *excellent* was used for the survey questions relating to their indicators to allow tourists to make better discriminations. Eighteen questions measured the five constructs in relation to assessment of overall satisfaction for the UK and Hong Kong. In Part 3, seven tourism-related service sectors were included: hotels, restaurants, retail shops, local tour operators, transport, visitor attractions, and immigration services. These services are commonly used by most Chinese tourists in both Hong Kong and the UK. Satisfaction with each sector's service was measured by three items in line with the overall satisfaction measurement in Parts 1 and 2. Part 4 included six questions regarding the respondent's gender, age, education, income, and frequency of visiting the UK and Hong Kong.

The target population of this survey was Mainland Chinese tourists who had visited both Hong Kong and the UK over the past 12 months. A face-to-face street intercept survey using a self-administered questionnaire was employed. A convenience sampling method was adopted. The surveys were carried out at popular tourist spots in the UK, such as city centers of Cambridge and Oxford; main attractions in London including Windsor Castle, the British Museum, Leicester Square, and Oxford Street, as well as two major outlet shopping centers in Portsmouth and Bicester Village. Once a potential respondent was approached, a filter question was asked: "Did you visit Hong Kong over the past 12 months?" The survey continued only if a positive answer was given. During 3 weeks of data collection in April 2010, over 230 Chinese tourists were interviewed. One hundred sixty-one responses were valid and contained less than 10% missing values and were thus used in this study.

Results and Analysis

The sample of 161 valid responses was used for the following analysis, including estimating two structural equation models (SEMs) for overall satisfaction with the UK and Hong Kong based on the theoretical model in Figure 1, followed by two SEMs that established the relationships between sectoral satisfaction and overall satisfaction. Overall TSIs and sectoral TSIs were then computed based on the above SEMs. Finally, statistical differences between the two sets of TSIs in relation to Hong Kong and the UK were respectively tested.

Demographic Profiles of the Sample

The demographic profiles of the survey respondents are presented in Table 1. As the table suggests, there was a good balance between male and female respondents; half were aged between 26 and 45; the majority (over 85%) of the respondents had a university level education or above; their average monthly household income was greater than 30,000 RMB; 41% were visiting the UK for the first time; and 63.4%

Table 1. Profile of Survey Respondents.

Variable	%
Sex	
Male	52.2
Female	47.8
Age	
16–25	21.1
26–35	28.0
36–45	24.2
46–55	18.6
56–65	3.7
≥ 66	4.3
Number of past visits to the UK	
0	41.0
1–3	40.4
4–6	6.2
7–9	1.2
≥ 10	11.2
Education	
No formal education	0.6
Primary/elementary school	0.6
Secondary/high school	12.4
College/university	54.0
Postgraduate	32.3
Monthly income (RMB)	
<7,000	14.3
7,000–20,999	36.0
21,000–34,999	23.0
35,000–48,999	5.6
49,000–69,999	11.2
$\geq 70,000$	9.9
Number of past visits to Hong Kong	
1–3	63.4
4–6	13.0
7–9	5.6
≥ 10	18.0

Note. All percentages were calculated on the basis of valid responses.

had visited Hong Kong no more than three times. This was a gender-balanced, mostly middle-aged, highly educated and relatively wealthy group of Mainland Chinese travelers with limited travel experience abroad.

Destination Satisfaction Analysis

The computer program Smart-PLS 2.0 M3 (Ringle et al., 2005) was employed to run SEMs. Both the inner (structural) and outer (measurement) models were estimated using the partial least squares (PLS) method. Because tourist surveys are usually subject to nonresponse, missing data needed to be imputed before estimating the model. The expectation–maximization (EM) algorithm in IBM SPSS 18 was employed to impute the missing values and obtain a complete data set. Model validity was assessed by determining the significance of the model's estimated path coefficients using the bootstrapping option, in line with Song et al. (2011, 2012).

Model Reduction

The original theoretical model of tourist satisfaction in Figure 1 is estimated for Hong Kong and the UK and the results (see Figures 2 and 3) showed high consistency with the results of Song et al. (2011). None of the path coefficients between the tourist characteristics construct and its consequences was significant for the UK or Hong Kong. This result indicates that these characteristics had little influence on tourist satisfaction, perceived performance, or assessed value. In line with Song et al. (2011, 2012), the tourist characteristics construct was removed from the model. In addition, the proposed

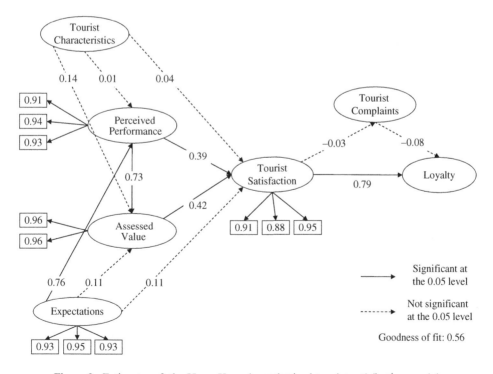

Figure 2. Estimates of the Hong Kong hypothesized tourist satisfaction model.

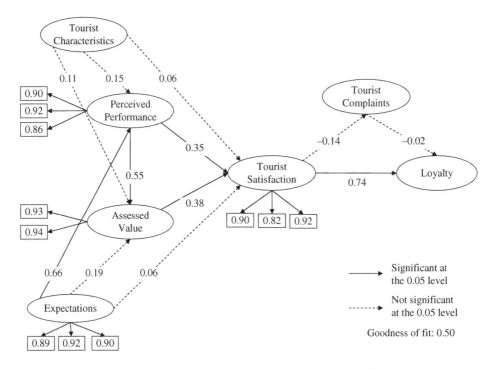

Figure 3. Estimates of the UK hypothesized tourist satisfaction model.

paths from tourist satisfaction to tourist complaints and from tourist complaints to loyalty were not significant for either destination. The nonsignificant path from tourist complaints to loyalty was consistent with the findings of Song et al. (2011, 2012). These findings suggest that tourist complaints do not have a significant mediating effect on the relationship between tourist satisfaction and loyalty. These findings can be explained by the fact that Chinese tourists lack an intention to complain. As Ap (2000) noted, Chinese tourists as well as some other Asian tourists tend to keep silent instead of expressing dissatisfaction to "save face" and to avoid embarrassing vendors. The tourist complaints construct was therefore removed from the model. The remaining path coefficients were highly consistent with the hypothesized model and were in line with the results of Song et al. (2011) in terms of statistical significance. After removing the tourist characteristics and tourist complaints constructs, the reduced model was reestimated and is assessed in the next section.

Reliability and Model Fit

The results of the final models were highly consistent with those of the original model regarding the values and significance levels of the remaining paths (see Tables 2–4 and Figures 4 and 5). As Figures 4 and 5 show, five out of seven paths were significant, with a coefficient above 0.30. These results suggest that the final model had strong predictive power and removing the tourist characteristics and tourist complaints constructs did not affect the reduced model's validity and power. A reliability analysis was conducted to test the level of internal consistency for the measurements of all of the reflective constructs. The indicators of the reflective constructs (tourist satisfaction, perceived

Table 2. Average Variance Extracted of Estimated Models.

Model	Satisfaction (%)	Performance (%)	Expectations (%)	Value (%)
Hong Kong hypothesized model	0.84	0.86	0.88	0.93
Hong Kong final model	0.85	0.86	0.88	0.93
UK hypothesized model	77.5	79.8	81.3	88.0
UK final model	77.5	79.8	81.3	88.1

Table 3. Cronbach's Alphas.

Model	Satisfaction	Performance	Expectations	Value
Hong Kong	0.90	0.92	0.93	0.92
The UK	0.86	0.87	0.89	0.86

Note. The results were the same for both the hypothesized and final models.

Table 4. Multiple R^2.

Model	Satisfaction	Performance	Value	Loyalty	Average
Hong Kong hypothesized model	0.76	0.58	0.71	0.64	0.67
Hong Kong final model	0.76	0.58	0.69	0.63	0.67
UK hypothesized model	0.53	0.49	0.53	0.55	0.53
UK final model	0.53	0.47	0.52	0.55	0.52

performance, expectations, assessed value) were reliable because all standardized indicator loadings in both the UK and Hong Kong models were positive and significant. Moreover, convergent validity of each reflective construct was evidenced by the average variances extracted (AVEs) in Table 2. For both estimated models, the AVEs were consistently above 75%, higher than the critical value of 50% as recommended by Fornell (1992). This indicates that each reflective dimension and its respective indicators were highly correlated (Chan et al., 2003). In addition, a substantial degree of internal consistency was evidenced by the high Cronbach's alphas, which ranged from 0.86 to 0.93 (see Table 3).

The R^2s for the structural equations used to predict tourist satisfaction were reasonably high for all models (see Table 4). The structural equations for predicting perceived performance, assessed value, and loyalty also presented reasonable explanatory power. To assess the overall model fit, a global fit measure for PLS path modeling introduced by Tenenhaus, Vinzi, Chatelin, and Lauro (2005) was calculated for each of the estimated models. The results are shown in Figures 2–5. The goodness-of-fit values ranged from 0.50 to 0.77, which all exceed the cutoff value of 0.36 for large effect sizes

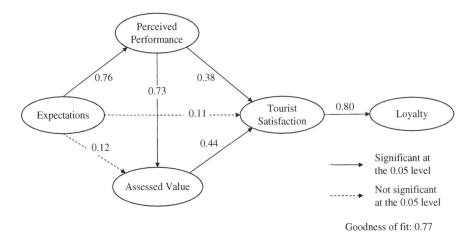

Figure 4. Path coefficients of the final Hong Kong tourist satisfaction model.

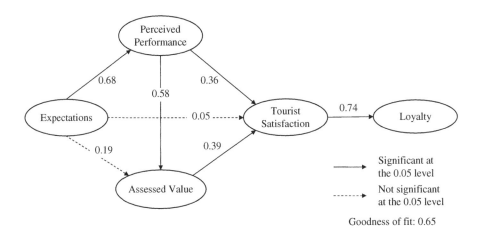

Figure 5. Path coefficients of the final UK tourist satisfaction model.

of R^2 (Wetzels, Odekerken-Schroder, & van Oppen, 2009). This suggests that both the hypothesized and reduced models performed well for both Hong Kong and the UK.

Comparisons between the estimation results of the original full model and the reduced final model for both Hong Kong and the UK (see Tables 2–4) showed that the reduced model had equal predictive power to the original one. Moreover, the reduced models showed higher goodness-of-fit values than the hypothesized ones in both cases. This suggests that the more parsimonious model is a valid and effective option. High consistency between the UK and Hong Kong model estimates and between this study and that of Song et al. (2011, 2012) suggests the general applicability of the theoretical model of the Hong Kong TSI. The main difference between the final model of this study and that of the Hong Kong TSI was on the tourist complaints construct. The removal of this construct was based on the statistical insignificance of both of its paths in the present study. This should be further verified in other empirical settings in the future.

Structural Relationships

The significant paths in Figures 4 and 5 suggest that perceived performance played a mediating role between expectations and tourist satisfaction and between expectations and assessed value. Tourists' initial expectations of various tourism services at a destination affected their evaluation of the received service performance, which in turn affected tourists' satisfaction level and their assessed value of the received services. In addition, perceived performance and assessed value both had positive and direct relationships with tourist satisfaction. The key role of perceived performance in tourists' satisfaction evaluation highlights the importance of improving service quality for destination competitiveness. Loyalty is a significant consequence of tourist satisfaction, and the estimated paths suggest a very strong correlation between tourist satisfaction and destination loyalty. Expectations showed no significant relationship with either assessed value or tourist satisfaction. Similar findings were reported in other studies (e.g., Chan et al., 2003; Johnson, Anderson, & Fornell, 1995).

Computation of Overall Destination TSIs

The overall destination TSI was computed using the model-implied weights (i.e., outer loadings of tourist satisfaction indicators in the estimated SEM). The TSI was then calculated as:

$$\text{TSI} = \frac{\omega_{\eta_{31}}\bar{y}_{31} + \omega_{\eta_{32}}\bar{y}_{32} + \omega_{\eta_{33}}\bar{y}_{33}}{\omega_{\eta_{31}} + \omega_{\eta_{32}} + \omega_{\eta_{33}}} \times 10, \tag{1}$$

where $\bar{y}_{31}$, $\bar{y}_{32}$, and $\bar{y}_{33}$ are the sample means of the three satisfaction indicators, and ω_{31}, ω_{32} and ω_{33} are the outer loadings. By multiplying a scaling constant 10 by the weighted average of the mean values of three satisfaction indicators, the calculated TSI is expressed on a 0–100 scale.

Based on the model estimates and the above formula, overall destination TSIs were computed for both Hong Kong and the UK, of 68.3 and 63.7, respectively. This result suggests that Mainland Chinese tourists were more satisfied with their tourism service experience in Hong Kong than in the UK.

Computation of Sectoral TSIs

In order to further examine Mainland Chinese tourists' satisfaction with individual tourism sectors in both Hong Kong and the UK and their contributions to the overall destination satisfaction, another SEM was established (see Figure 6). In this model, tourist satisfaction with each of the seven tourism-related sectors (i.e., hotels, restaurants, visitor attractions, retail shops, transport, local tour operators, and immigration services) was included as an antecedent of overall destination satisfaction. The path coefficients represent the contribution of sector-level satisfaction to the overall evaluation of destination satisfaction.

It should be noted that not all proposed path coefficients were expected to be significant, because not all service encounters at a destination affect a tourist's overall satisfaction significantly. The significant path coefficients were expected to have a positive sign given the positive correlation between sector-level satisfaction and overall

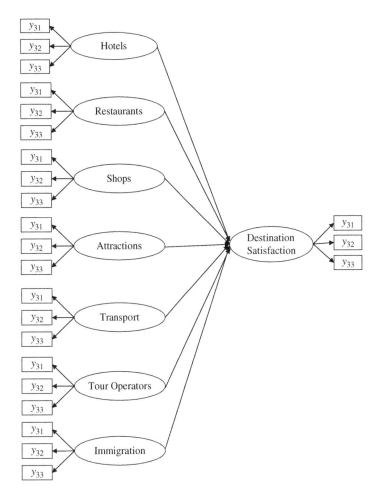

Figure 6. Sector-level satisfaction model.

destination satisfaction. The outer loadings of each sector's satisfaction indicators were used to compute this sector's TSI based on Formula (1).

The estimation results are presented in Table 5 and Figures 7 and 8. Table 5 indicates that the estimated models were satisfactory. The indicators of all constructs were reliable as all standardized indicator loadings in both the Hong Kong and UK models were positive and significant. For both models estimated, the AVEs were consistently well above the critical value of 50%. In addition, a substantial degree of internal consistency was evidenced by the high Cronbach's alphas, which were all above 0.80.

Figures 7 and 8 suggest that three tourism-related service sectors were significantly related to Mainland Chinese tourists' overall satisfaction with both Hong Kong and the UK. These were visitor attractions, hotels, and local tour operators. The relatively high contribution of visitor attractions' satisfaction to the overall satisfaction assessment can be explained by the fact that the primary purpose of most Mainland Chinese visitors in Hong Kong and the UK was leisure and sightseeing. Therefore, visiting well-known visitor attractions accounted for a major part of their travel experiences in the UK and Hong Kong. This was particularly true for first-time visitors. Accommodation is one of

Table 5. Estimation Results for Sector-Level Satisfaction Models.

	Hotels	Restaurants	Shops	Attractions	Transport	Tour Operators	Immigration Services
Hong Kong model							
AVE	77.2	78.3	79.6	78.4	78.3	82.3	76.0
Alpha	0.85	0.86	0.87	0.86	0.86	0.89	0.84
Destination satisfaction $R^2 = 0.61$							
UK model							
AVE	82.1	76.9	75.6	78.6	76.6	75.4	74.9
Alpha	0.89	0.85	0.84	0.86	0.85	0.84	0.83
Destination satisfaction $R^2 = 0.49$							

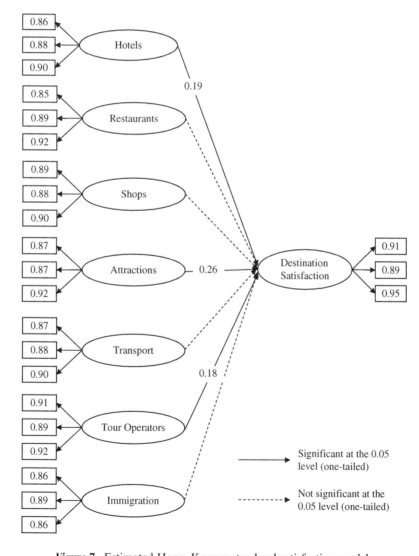

Figure 7. Estimated Hong Kong sector-level satisfaction model.

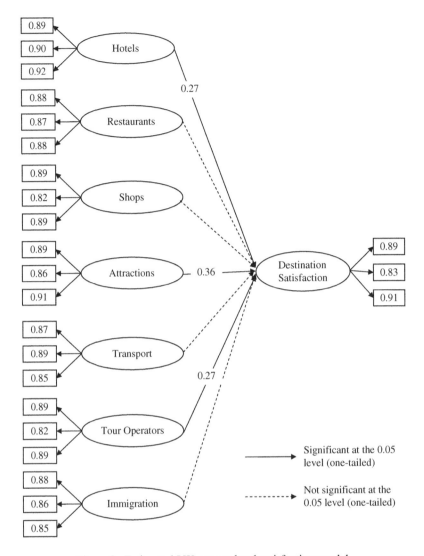

Figure 8. Estimated UK sector-level satisfaction model.

the primary and necessary elements of travel and tourism and therefore plays an important role in tourists' overall satisfaction. Due to language barriers and visa restrictions, most Chinese tourists joined guided tours when traveling overseas. Thus, they had close contacts with tour guides throughout their trip. The service quality of the tour operator is therefore important for their overall satisfaction evaluation.

The computed sector-level TSIs for Hong Kong and the UK and their ranks are reported in Table 6. With respect to Hong Kong, Mainland Chinese tourists were most satisfied with public transport services, followed by retail shops and immigration services, and least satisfied with local tour operators, followed by hotels. The efficient, cost-effective, and clean public transport system in Hong Kong is widely recognized by all international tourists. Shopping in Hong Kong is one of the key motivations of Chinese tourists. A good variety of international brands and reasonable prices, well-

Table 6. Computed Sectoral and Overall TSIs for Hong Kong and the UK.

	Hong Kong	UK
Visitor attractions	66.2 [5]	66.3 [1]
Hotels	64.6 [6]	54.4 [7]
Tour operators	63.1 [7]	60.4 [4]
Restaurants	68.1 [3=]	56.3 [6]
Retail shops	68.3 [2]	62.2 [3]
Transport	70.3 [1]	65.1 [2]
Immigration services	68.1 [3=]	58.0 [5]
Overall	68.3	63.7

Note. Figures in brackets refer to the ranks of sectoral TSIs for each destination.
     [3=], third position.

developed shopping facilities, together with language barrier-free service staff satisfied their shopping desires. The efficiency of immigration services and the staff's Mandarin language skills left a very positive first impression once they arrived in Hong Kong. On the other hand, the relatively low satisfaction score for local tour operators can be explained by the phenomenon of discounted tour packages. The highly discounted or even "zero-fee" tour packages result in a trade-off between low-quality accommodation and visits to high-priced souvenir and jewelry shops. This may also partially explain the relatively low satisfaction score of the hotel sector.

As far as the UK tourism sectors are concerned, Mainland Chinese tourists were most satisfied with visitor attractions in the UK, followed by transport and retail shops, but least satisfied with hotels, followed by restaurant services. High satisfaction with attractions in the UK was confirmed by other studies regarding both culturally and geographically distant destinations of Chinese tourists (Li & Carr, 2004; Ryan & Mo, 2001). This can be explained by tourists' novelty-seeking motives. However, this finding does not mean that tourists would necessarily have low satisfaction with the attractions at a geographically or culturally close destination. Such a destination may also offer tourists some novel experiences, such as Hong Kong Disneyland. This may explain their high satisfaction with attractions in Hong Kong as well. Low satisfaction with hotels in both destinations was in line with past relevant literature (Heung, 2000; Wang et al., 2008). Language barriers seem to be a key issue particularly in those service encounters that require more human contact and oral communication, such as retail shops, restaurants, and hotels. Some designer fashion stores in London and key shopping outlets in the UK have hired Mandarin-speaking shop assistants, and therefore the language barriers have been mostly overcome. This contributes to Chinese tourists' relatively high satisfaction with the UK retail sector, compared to restaurant and hotel sectors where Chinese-speaking employees are still rare.

As discussed above, visitor attractions, hotels, and tour operators are most relevant to Mainland Chinese tourists' overall assessments of destination satisfaction. The hotel sector was ranked low in both destinations. Visitor attractions in the UK seem to be particularly appealing to Mainland Chinese tourists, which contribute the most to their overall satisfaction. On the other hand, attention should be paid to tour operator services in Hong Kong.

Comparisons of TSIs Between Hong Kong and the UK

The above sections have presented the computed overall destination TSIs and sectoral TSIs for both Hong Kong and the UK. In addition to the visitor attraction sector, Mainland Chinese tourists were more satisfied with tourism-related services in Hong Kong than in the UK (see Table 6). In particular, Mainland Chinese tourists' satisfaction scores for hotels, restaurants, and immigration services were more than 10 points higher than those for the UK counterparts. These findings can be partially explained by travel motivation theories. Weiermair and Fuchs (2000) argued that tourist behavior is driven by two contradictory motives: novel experiences and habitual experiences. *Novelty seeking* relates to new services, products, attractions, or exotic destinations, and *habitual tourism behavior* refers to the continuation of old habits, preferences, and activities experienced in everyday life, such as food preferences and eating habits. It can be argued that a tourist often has both motives during a single trip. He or she may pursue exotic cultural experiences at a new destination but maintain his or her eating habits. Regarding food and accommodation, most Chinese tourists may pursue habitual experiences during travel, and food and accommodation in Hong Kong are more similar to what they are accustomed to and therefore more satisfactory compared to those in the UK. Novelty-seeking motives may apply to the experience with some exotic attractions, such as cultural/historical heritage and theme amusement parks. Because both the UK and Hong Kong offer some attractions to meet Chinese tourists' novelty-seeking needs, their satisfaction levels were almost equally high. However, compared to other sectors at the same destination, Chinese tourists' satisfaction with visitor attractions was ranked much higher in the UK than in Hong Kong, first and fifth, respectively. In this sense it can be argued that the UK does comparably better in offering Chinese tourists novel experiences. The following section provides statistical evidence of the differences between these two sets of TSIs.

Paired *t*-tests were employed to investigate whether Mainland Chinese tourists' satisfaction with each tourism-related service sector and the destination as a whole was significantly different between Hong Kong and the UK. Although only three sectors' satisfaction levels were significantly related to the overall satisfaction evaluation, it was still useful to make comparisons across all seven sectors between the two destinations, given the managerial implications for each of the sectors under comparison. Table 7 presents the results of statistical tests. For the only sector where Mainland Chinese tourists were more satisfied in the UK than in Hong Kong—that is, visitor attractions—the satisfaction gap between the two destinations was not statistically significant. The same

Table 7. Statistical Tests of TSI Differences Between Hong Kong and the UK.

	$TSI_{HK} - TSI_{UK}$	*T*-statistic	*p*-Value
Visitor attractions	−0.1	−0.07	.94
Hotels	10.2	6.30	.00
Tour operators	2.7	1.66	.10
Restaurants	11.8	7.33	.00
Retail shops	6.1	4.58	.00
Transport	5.2	3.54	.00
Immigration services	10.1	6.05	.00
Overall	4.6	3.08	.00

was found when comparing satisfaction with tour operators. For the other five sectors as well as the overall evaluation, Hong Kong received significantly higher satisfaction scores than the UK. These findings suggest that Hong Kong has greater tourism competitiveness over the UK as far as the Mainland Chinese tourist market is concerned.

Concluding Remarks

This study aimed to compare Mainland Chinese tourists' satisfaction with Hong Kong and the UK based on a newly developed TSI framework. The theoretical model of tourist satisfaction was tested at the destination level. The empirical results were highly consistent with the previous studies of Song et al. (2011, 2012) based on the same model. The unique research design of such a comparative setting further suggests the wide applicability of the TSI theoretical model.

This study computed the overall destination TSIs and sectoral TSIs for both Hong Kong and the UK (see Figure 9 for a summary). On the whole, Mainland Chinese tourists were more satisfied with Hong Kong than with the UK as their travel destination. With respect to individual service sectors, Mainland Chinese tourists were most satisfied with transport services and least satisfied with local tour operators in Hong Kong. Visitor attractions in the UK received the highest satisfaction score among the seven sectors and hotels received the lowest score. Among the seven sectors considered, visitor attractions, hotels, and local tour operators showed the most significant contributions to Mainland Chinese tourists' overall destination satisfaction for both destinations. A comparison between the two destinations suggests that Mainland Chinese tourists were more satisfied with six out of seven tourism-related service sectors in Hong Kong than in the UK. In particular, the TSIs for restaurants, immigration services, and hotels in Hong Kong were more than 10 points higher than the TSIs for their UK counterparts.

The above findings suggest that Hong Kong's tourism industry has gained more competitiveness over the UK as far as Mainland Chinese tourists are concerned. This can be explained by the fact that many tourism and hospitality operators in Hong Kong have adopted industry-wide and/or internationally recognized service standards to

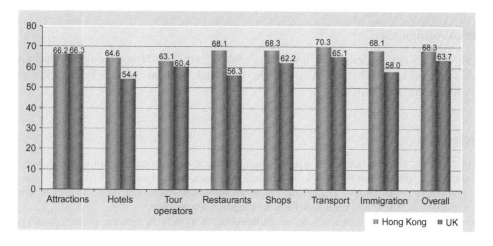

Figure 9. Comparison of Hong Kong and UK TSIs (color figure available online).

ensure a high level of service, and particular effort has been made in understanding and satisfying this critical market, such as hiring Mandarin-speaking service staff. In comparison, language barriers and cultural differences were more prominent in tourism sectors in the UK as a more culturally distant destination for Chinese tourists. Given the potential negative relationship between cultural distance and tourist satisfaction, tourism service providers in both Hong Kong and the UK should continue to improve their understanding of the cultural characteristics of the Chinese tourist market and adopt cross-cultural perspectives in their operations. Service providers need to be more aware of and sensitive to cultural differences. Relevant staff training including inter-cultural communication skills is necessary. Cultural knowledge will contribute to both service providers' business success and international tourists' satisfaction with their experience in intercultural encounters.

It should be noted that this study has a few limitations. First of all, the empirical study was based on a relatively small sample and the convenience sampling method, which may affect generalization of the findings. A larger scale of the study with a similar comparative setting should be considered. Secondly, the research design of this study was slightly different from the studies by Song et al. (2011, 2012), although the theoretical model and methodology were highly consistent. Thus, caution should be exercised when interpreting the results of this study in comparison to Song et al. (2011, 2012). As a comparative study, this article focuses on destination-level satisfaction to test the theoretical model, and only the tourist satisfaction construct was measured in relation to each tourism sector in the survey. The different research design and focus did not allow direct comparison of the computed TSIs at both the destination and sector levels with those of Song et al. (2011, 2012). Lastly, the survey was conducted in the UK, but the respondents had also visited Hong Kong no more than 12 months before. Thus, it can be argued that these respondents had clearer memories about their service encounters in the UK than those in Hong Kong. Because it would be extremely difficult to track tourists and conduct the survey with the same population of respondents in both Hong Kong and the UK, this limitation is unavoidable for such a comparative study, although effort has been made to minimize the bias, such as omitting any response with over 10% missing values.

Acknowledgment

The authors acknowledge the financial support from The Hong Kong Polytechnic University (Grant No. 1-ZVA5) and the National Natural Science Foundation of China (Grant No. 71103206).

References

Ap, J. (2000). Understanding the Asian respondent when conducting tourism research: Some challenges, pitfalls and tips. In N. Nickerson, N. Mosey, & K. Andereck (Eds.), *31st Annual Conference Proceedings, Travel and Tourism Research Association* (pp. 282–290). San Fernando Valley, CA: Travel and Tourism Research Association.

Boulding, W., Kalra, A., Staeling, R., & Zeithaml, V. A. (1993). A dynamic process model of service quality: From expectations to behavioral intentions. *Journal of Marketing Research, 30*(2), 7–27.

Chan, L. K., Hui, Y. V., Lo, H. P., Tse, S. K., Tso, K. F., & Wu, M. L. (2003). Consumer satisfaction index: New practice and findings. *European Journal of Marketing, 37*(5/6), 872–909.

Chon, K. (2005, December). Opening address for the second China Tourism Forum and the third China Tourism Academy annual conference, Kunming, China.

Fornell, C. (1992). A national customer satisfaction barometer: The Swedish experience. *Journal of Marketing, 56*(1), 6–21.

Fuchs, M., & Weiermair, K. (2004). Destination benchmarking: An indicator-system's potential for exploring guest satisfaction. *Journal of Travel Research, 42*(3), 212–225.

Grönroos, C. (1984). A service quality model and its marketing implications. *European Journal of Marketing, 18*(4), 36–44.

Henning-Thurau, T., & Klee, A. (1997). The impact of customer satisfaction and relationship quality on customer retention: A critical reassessment and model development. *Psychology and Marketing, 14*(8), 737–764.

Heung, V. C. S. (2000). Satisfaction levels of Mainland Chinese travellers with Hong Kong hotel services. *International Journal of Contemporary Hospitality Management, 12*(5), 308–315.

Hong Kong Tourism Board. (2011). *A statistical review of Hong Kong tourism 2010.* Hong Kong SAR, China: Author.

Johnson, M. D., Anderson, E. W., & Fornell, C. (1995). Rational and adaptive performance expectations in a customer satisfaction framework. *Journal of Consumer Research, 21*(4), 28–40.

Kau, A. K., & Lim, P. S. (2005). Clustering of Chinese tourists to Singapore: An analysis of their motivations, values and satisfaction. *International Journal of Tourism Research, 7*(4–5), 231–248.

Kozak, M., & Rimmington, M. (2000). Tourist satisfaction with Mallorca, Spain, as an off-season holiday destination. *Journal of Travel Research, 38*(3), 260–269.

Li, J. W. J., & Carr, N. (2004). Visitor satisfaction: An analysis of Mainland Chinese tourists on the Australian Gold Coast. *International Journal of Hospitality and Tourism Administration, 5*(3), 31–48.

Oh, H., & Parks, S. C. (1997). Customer satisfaction and service quality: A critical review of the literature and research implications for the hospitality industry. *Hospitality Research Journal, 20*(3), 35–64.

Oliver, R. L. (1980). A cognitive model of the antecedents and consequences of satisfaction decisions. *Journal of Marketing Research, 17*(4), 460–469.

Parasuraman, A., Zeithaml, V. A., & Berry, L. L. (1985). A concept model of service quality and its implications for future research. *Journal of Marketing, 49*(3), 41–50.

Qu, H., & Li, L. (1997). The characteristics and satisfaction of Mainland Chinese visitors to Hong Kong. *Journal of Travel Research, 35*(4), 31–41.

Ringle, C. M., Wende, S., & Will, A. (2005). SmartPLS – Version 2.0. Retrieved from http://www.smartpls.de. Hamburg, Germany: SmartPLS.

Ryan, C., & Mo, X. (2001). Chinese visitors to New Zealand—Demographics and perceptions. *Journal of Vacation Marketing, 8*(1), 13–27.

Sirgy, M. J. (1984). A social cognition model of consumer satisfaction/dissatisfaction: An experiment. *Psychology and Marketing, 1*(2), 27–44.

Song, H., Li, G., van der Veen, R., & Chen, J. L. (2011). Assessing Mainland Chinese tourists' satisfaction with Hong Kong using the tourist satisfaction index. *International Journal of Tourism Research, 13*(1), 82–96.

Song, H., van der Veen, R., Li, G., & Chen, J. L. (2012). Hong Kong tourist satisfaction index. *Annals of Tourism Research, 39*(1), 459–479.

Tenenhaus, M., Vinzi, V. E., Chatelin, Y. M., & Lauro, C. (2005). PLS path modeling. *Computational Statistics & Data Analysis, 48*(1), 159–205.

United Nations World Tourism Organization. (1999). *World tourism organization tourism vision 2020.* Madrid, Spain: Author.

United Nations World Tourism Organization. (2003). *China outbound tourism*. Madrid, Spain: Author.

VisitBritain. (2010a). *Overseas visitors to Britain: Understanding trends, attitudes and characteristics*. London, England: Author.

VisitBritain. (2010b). *Written evidence from VisitBritain (TE 26)*. Retrieved from http://www.publications.parliament.uk/pa/cm201011/cmselect/cmtran/473/473we16.htm

VisitBritain. (2012). *Market and trade profile: China*. London, England: Author.

Wang, Y., & Davidson, M. C. G. (2010). Pre- and post-trip perceptions: An insight into Chinese package holiday market to Australia. *Journal of Vacation Marketing, 16*(2), 111–123.

Wang, Y., Vela, M. R., & Tyler, K. (2008). Cultural perspectives: Chinese perceptions of UK hotel service quality. *International Journal of Culture, Tourism and Hospitality Research, 2*(4), 312–329.

Weiermair, K., & Fuchs, M. (2000). The impact of cultural distance on perceived service quality gaps. *Journal of Quality Assurance in Hospitality and Tourism, 1*(2), 59–75.

Wetzels, M., Odekerken-Schroder, G., & van Oppen, C. (2009). Using PLS path modeling for assessing hierarchical construct models: Guidelines and empirical illustration. *MIS Quarterly, 33*(1), 177–195.

Wong, J., & Law, R. (2003). Difference in shopping satisfaction levels: A study of tourists in Hong Kong. *Tourism Management, 24*(4), 401–410.

Yi, Y. (1990). A critical review of consumer satisfaction. In V. A. Zeithaml (Ed.), *Review of marketing* (pp. 68–123). Birmingham, AL: American Marketing Association.

Yoon, Y., & Uysal, M. (2005). An examination of the effects of motivation and satisfaction on destination loyalty: A structural model. *Tourism Management, 26*(1), 45–56.

Zhang, G., Song, R., & Liu, D. (Eds.). (2011). *Green book of China's tourism 2011: China's tourism development analysis and forecast*. Heide, Germany: China Outbound Tourism Research Institute.

Annoying Tourist Behaviors: Perspectives of Hosts and Tourists in Macao

以澳门居民及游客的观点探讨恼人的旅客行为

KIM IENG LOI
PHILIP L. PEARCE

The study of annoying tourist behaviors is timely as key destinations in Asia welcome large waves of new arrivals. In this study in Macao, 728 respondents—half of whom were tourists and the other half local residents—provided ratings of the perceived frequency and levels of annoyance of 40 potentially problematic behaviors. The behaviors studied were identified by a two-step, inclusive, emic and conceptually driven process and classified with a new framework. The results provided evidence that a few select behaviors (smoking in public, spitting and littering, not flushing toilets, abusing service personnel) were both highly annoying and frequent. An action grid was developed to illustrate the behaviors across these two measurements. Most undesirable behaviors studied are not yet widely prevailing in Macao but these annoying behaviors could pose potential threat to stakeholders as the number of tourist arrivals continued to increase. The authors also linked the findings with numerous theories in the literature including those of cultural convergence, personal relevance, and self-serving biases in attribution. Communities seeking to manage less desirable behaviors can build their strategies based on these kinds of empirical findings.

到访亚洲主要目的地的旅客人数不断增加，关于旅客恼人行为的研究变得非常必要。本研究在澳门进行，调查了七百二十八位受访者，其中旅客和当地居民各占一半。受访人士就他们对四十项潜在的问题行为的感知频率和干扰程度作出评价。我们以二步、包容性的、主位及概念驱动的过程找出问题行为，并以新的框架将之分类。结果显示，受访者认为以下行为是非常恼人和常见的，包括在公共场所吸烟、随地吐痰和乱抛垃圾、不冲厕所及侮辱服务人员。大部分不受欢迎的行为在澳门尚不十分普遍，但随着游客人数持续上升，这些恼人行为将对利益相关者构成潜在威胁。此外，作者将本文的研究结果结合有关文献进行了探讨，包括文化趋同、个人关联及自利归因偏误等理论，各个地方亦可借鉴本文的研究成果来制定合适的管理不受欢迎行为的策略。

关键词：恼人的旅客行为，澳门，主客观点，意义的协调管理，个人关联

Kim Ieng Loi is Assistant Professor at the Institute for Tourism Studies in Macao, Macao SAR, China.

Philip L. Pearce is a Foundation Professor of Tourism at James Cook University, Townsville, Australia.

Introduction

Tourist behavior is a well-researched topic (Bowen & Clarke, 2009; Kozak & DeCrop, 2009; Morgan, Lugosi, & Ritchie, 2010; P. L. Pearce, 2005, 2011a; Pizam & Mansfeld, 2000). Many tourist behavior studies focus on pre-arrival behaviors such as destination choice and how to devise marketing strategies by understanding such decision-making processes (Buhalis, 2000; Johns, 2002; Mansfeld, 1992; Oppermann, 1999; Seddighi & Theocharous, 2002). Those studies focusing on tourists' on-destination behaviors often have an orientation toward eco-tourism (Grossberg, Treves, & Naughton-Treves, 2003; Jacobson & Lopez, 1994; Orams & Hill, 1998) and heritage sites (Brown, 1999; Moscardo, 1996). Some researchers, when studying responsible/civilized/ethical tourist behaviors, have focused on cross-nationality comparisons rather than the behaviors per se (Pizam, Jansen-Verbeke, & Steel, 1997). There appear to be no studies that have attempted to investigate undesirable tourist behaviors from the joint perspectives of both tourists and hosts, which is a desirable research direction because both groups are directly influenced by such behaviors (Moscardo, 1996). There is thus a relatively untapped topic area relating to the perceptions of desirable and undesirable tourist behaviors.

The popular press and less formal literature have contributed to the identification of undesirable tourist behaviors as a topic of widespread interest. In 2002, Expedia, Microsoft's online travel service, conducted a survey in which tourist offices from 17 popular destinations worldwide were asked to vote on their least favorite tourists (BBC News, 2002). Expedia carried out a similar online survey in 2009, collecting opinions on the best travelers overall, as well as on specific categories such as politeness, generosity, behavior, and the propensity to complain (Business Standard, 2012). Japanese, British, and Canadian tourists were ranked as the top three best behaved tourists, and the French were voted as the world's worst tourists (Business Standard, 2012). Other popular literature, such as the work of Blackden (2004), who collated some of his personal encounters of shocking behaviors by tourists abroad into a book, has offered lists of offensive acts and actions. Though these efforts help to highlight the importance of studying tourists' on-site behaviors (in particular the less-than-desirable ones), the systematic consideration of how tourists and communities react to key behaviors requires more empirical work.

The context for this study is China's special administrative region of Macao, which functions as a popular tourism destination for the developing waves of travelers within Asia. The actions and activities of international tourists in Macao (and especially Mainland Chinese tourists) form a behavioral test case of the acceptability and frequency of select tourist behaviors. The purpose of the study is to consider empirically the popular concerns about the acceptability and good conduct of international tourists. In particular, it can be argued that many Mainland Chinese travelers are on the cusp of learning how to be global tourism citizens (Arnold, 2005; Chen, 2011; *China Daily*, 2006; Zeng, 2006; Zhang, 2006). This view is supported by formal Chinese government documents such as that from the Office of the Spiritual Civilisation Steering Committee, which in 2006 released a listing of "do's and do not's" for Mainland citizens intending to travel abroad (Chio, 2010). An overview of these behavioral issues is presented first at a general level through the use of a frequency–annoyance action grid similar to the importance–performance matrix, followed by a second phase through linking the behaviors to three new themed categories identified by the authors. The new themed categories are:

1. behaviors directly relating to others;
2. isolated individual acts, which are subdivided into

   a. bodily functions or presentation/appearance issues; and
   b. verbal or sound acts; and

3. marginally illegal or scam behaviors.

These categories were inspired by previous efforts in cross-cultural communication on gaze and reverse gaze (Maoz, 2006) and the coordinated management of meaning (CMM) approach, which considers speech and sound acts, key episodes, relationship interactions, views of the self in relation to society, and broad cultural patterns (Pearce Associates, 1999; B. Pearce, 2005; Philipsen, 1995).

In this way, the study fulfills two interesting goals: it (a) systematically records a set of behaviors that are structured according to a new coding framework; and (b) notes how problematic tourist behaviors are perceived by both tourists and hosts. The work is linked to contemporary conceptual directions of how travelers adopt new roles and behaviors as they move away from their home circumstances and view fresh worlds (Seaton, 2002).

Literature Review

As briefly noted in the Introduction, there are several threads of inquiry concerning the on-site study of tourist behaviors. There is a body of descriptive work concerned with direct observation, which involves recording what people do and for how long they do it. Some of the earliest work in this tradition comes from museum studies by Robinson (as cited in Bell, Fisher, & Loomis, 1978) and Melton (1933, 1936, 1972). The growth of these kinds of studies has been limited and they are mainly conducted in zoos and confined spaces where tracking and watching visitors is a manageable research task (Bitgood, 2003, 2006). Additionally, there are studies on the perception of the meaning and explanations of what tourists do, and this area of inquiry includes the views of other tourists, tour guides, members of host communities, and tourism business employees (cf. P. L. Pearce, Moscardo, & Ross, 1996; Pizam, 1999a, 1999b). A third area of interest is the work on how to influence and change tourist behaviors. In these kinds of studies, researchers typically present ideas and discuss and evaluate strategies aimed at improving social interaction and learning among interacting parties (Falk, Ballantyne, Packer, & Benckendorff, 2012; Ward, Bochner, & Furnham, 2001). A further perspective on these areas of inquiry is provided by the concept of *people watching*, which has diverse and deep roots (Collett, 2004). Prior to the development of social science analysis, literary and philosophical commentators portrayed many of the foibles and follies of public behaviors (cf. Argyle, 1975; D. Morris, 1985). Anthropologists and sociologists conducted the early social science observational work on human societies (Goffman, 1959; Malinowski, 1922/2006). Their studies highlighted the value of keeping detailed records and tracking what people did as well as what they said about their worlds. In studying animal behavior, ethologists contributed to the practice of good observational analysis (Ball, 2004; Eibl-Eibesfeldt, 1989; Hinde, 1972). Clearly, animals do not speak, so the ethologists' efforts to study animal behavior relied exclusively on careful observation. The legacy of this work for the present study lies in being thorough in identifying the activities to be considered, such as initially using open-ended rather than closed-ended recording approaches. All of these areas of inquiry are relevant to the present study because the work builds from the identification of problematic tourist behaviors to a more detailed study of the perceptions of the desirability of those behaviors. Such work has potential implications for the management of select kinds of annoying actions. Some highlights and methodological implications from the previous work warrant further attention to provide a full context for the present aims and research effort.

There are several other subtle issues involved in any simple observation of tourist behaviors. Different individuals will identify diverse behaviors as problematic due to their alternate interpretations of whether the behavior is intentional or not. M. W. Morris and Mason (2009), in a detailed analysis of how we interpret observable behavior, argued that if we see the behavior as intentional we think like storytellers and suggest motives and reasons and embellish the observed behavior with personality descriptions. For behavior that we see as unintentional, typically we reason abstractly like scientists and discount the personal issues and resort to situational explanations. These considerations direct researchers to the need to establish how members of a community rate and see behavior. We cannot automatically assume that a given behavior will be seen the same way or cause the same kind of offense as might be apparent to a researcher. Additionally, the cultural variability in public behaviors adds a further level of complexity to the study of public acts and reinforces the need to obtain large samples of residents who can adjudicate on these acceptability issues from a common cultural perspective (Reisinger & Turner, 2003).

Another related area of concern and debate regarding the study and interpretation of tourist behaviors lies in the value of using nationality as a key explanatory variable. Dann (1993) initiated the debate in tourism study and expressed the view that due to rising globalization and the diversity that exists within cultures, simply using nationality labels is likely to risk gross overgeneralization of the forces driving public behavior. Pizam and Sussman (1995) and Pizam et al. (1997) argued that it is pragmatic to use the classification of nationality because many sectors of the industry treat their tourists on this basis and it does have a value in describing group differences. The position adopted in this research is that nationality will be considered as a background rather than a foreground issue for the study. The focus will be on the converging or diverging perception between tourists and hosts in terms of what they see as less desirable behaviors rather than identifying national groups who regularly produce the identified behaviors. There are both academic as well as pragmatic reasons for this focus on the behaviors. In research terms we do not want to suggest that all members of a nationality consistently exhibit some of the identified undesirable behaviors. It has already been noted that some governments, including the Chinese government, do specifically give advice to their citizens on how to behave. Nevertheless, from a destination management perspective, the advice about desirable behavior might appear racist or discriminatory if targeted at one nationality and because undesirable behaviors may be widespread in terms of the nationalities of those exhibiting these acts, it is pragmatic to frame communications in a generic way rather than targeting any one source region.

Studying the perception and views of both tourists and residents is an important consideration for tourism management. For tourism development to be sustainable, the host population must be favorably disposed to it (Loukissas, 1993; Ross, 1991). Many researchers have acknowledged the importance of taking into consideration the perception and attitudes of both tourists and hosts in tourism studies (Allen, Long, Perdue, & Kieselbach, 1988; Caneday & Zeiger, 1991; Jurowski, Uysal, & Williams, 1997;

Kavallins & Pizam, 1994; Lawson, William, Young, & Cossens, 1998; Payne & Dimanche, 1996; P. L. Pearce, 1995; Ryan, Scotland, & Montgomery, 1998). However, for the present purposes, conventional analysis of the host–guest contact is too broad (Smith, 1989), because it usually focuses on macro issues such as perceived large-scale impacts brought about by tourism (or the movement of tourists; Dogan, 1989; Inskeep, 1991; Milman & Pizam, 1988; Murphy, 1985; Pizam, 1978; Smith, 1989). No studies reviewed thus far have tried to investigate the more micro aspect of the (dis)similar perspectives of these two important stakeholder groups in relation to less-than-desirable tourist behaviors in general.

These perspectives and issues from the literature help frame some of the methods as well as sharpen the aims of the present study. The overarching aim of the study may be articulated as follows: the present research seeks to assess the perceived frequency and levels of annoyance of tourist behaviors in Macao. The topic will be approached with sensitivity to not targeting particular nationality groups exhibiting these behaviors to avoid potential discrimination. The sources of the behaviors to be studied will be derived from the previous literature but, importantly, these behavioral acts will be supplemented by adding contributions from the local citizens. The assessment of the perceived frequency and levels of annoyances will be approached from both tourists' and hosts' perspectives based on newly developed categories incorporating respondents' views of the behaviors that matter. The nationality of those exhibiting the behaviors will not be directly examined, although it is recognized that the dominant tourist group to Macao is Mainland Chinese tourists.

Methodology, Sampling, and Instrumentation

The study of the perceived annoyance and frequency of tourist behaviors was approached in two phases. Using a structured approach built on previous work identifying cross-culturally challenging tourist behaviors as well as personal observation, a list of potentially problematic acts and actions was constructed (Collett, 2004; Cronen & Shuter, 1983; P. L. Pearce, 1995; P. L. Pearce, Kim, & Lussa, 1998). In this first stage, the list of undesirable tourist behaviors was not shown to the respondents. Rather, respondents were asked for some annoying behaviors in an open question format. They were then prompted for more answers by being shown the prepared list. As a result, a list of undesirable tourist behaviors deemed relevant by a sample of 240 residents and 240 tourists in Macao was systematically constructed. The demographic characteristics of this pilot sample closely resembled that of the main sample, which will be discussed in the later section titled "Demographics of the Sample". The relatively large sample size as a pilot study in this first emic phase of research provided a sound foundation, based on which a final list of behaviors was constructed and effectively delivered to 840 respondents in the second phase. Eventually 728 forms were satisfactorily completed. Again the views of both local Macao residents and visiting tourists were assessed with (a) the frequency of the behaviors recorded and (b) a rating of how annoying the behaviors were deemed to be.

Sampling

To achieve the final sample of 728 respondents (as well as the 480 respondents in the first phase of the pilot study), a common pool of university students seasoned in conducting street interviews was recruited and they randomly intercepted respondents in major tourist areas in Macao with a requirement of collecting an even distribution of visitors and residents. A total of 840 interviews were conducted at the end of April and in early May 2011. Because there were 40 statements and two questions for each statement, 40 pairs of responses were obtained from each respondent. However, due to the length of the questionnaire, some respondents opted out before full completion of the questionnaire. A criterion of no more than 10% missing values was applied to screen out unusable response sets; that is, all responses with more than four pairs of questions unanswered were deleted from the sample. With this criterion applied, a total of 728 effective responses were included in the analysis in this article.

Instrumentation

A total of 40 cross-culturally challenging tourist behaviors were identified from the first phase and included in the final questionnaire. Respondents were asked two questions about each behavior:

1. In general, how frequently do you come across the following behavior?
2. How annoying is the following behavior to you whenever you come across it?

Evaluation was made based on an ordinal 4-point scale: 1 (*never encountered before/not at all annoying*), 2 (*not very frequently/mildly annoying*), 3 (*somewhat frequently/quite annoying*) and 4 (*very frequently/very annoying*). Demographic information was also solicited.

Demographics of the Sample

The 728 effective responses were collected during a 7-day survey period from April 28 to May 4, 2011. This survey period was selected because it fell into one of the three traditional peak tourist seasons, which are commonly known as the *Golden Weeks* in Macao. These peak periods are the result of China's labor laws, which require most citizens to take their vacations around three major holidays: the Lunar New Year holiday in late January and early February; Labor Day on May 1; and National Day on October 1. Each of these periods initiates a week-long vacation period called the Golden Week (Arnold, 2005). Although the Chinese government modified the Golden Week arrangement in 2008 to break it into shorter breaks and to cancel the May 1 Golden Week, this period is still considered to be a time of high tourist movement and activities.

Table 1 shows the demographic characteristics of the respondents. The even distribution of residents ($N = 363$, 49.9%) and tourists ($N = 365$, 50.1%) was purposeful for the sake of intergroup comparison. There were slightly more female respondents than male respondents (53 and 47%, respectively), and this reflected the population characteristics; the latest demographic information released by the Macao government revealed that males and females account for 48.0 and 52.0% of the total population, respectively (Macao Statistics and Census Service, 2012a). The respondents were mainly 15–44 years old (84.2%) with high school or vocational training (39.97%) or a bachelor's degree or above (50.96%). Most were from Mainland China (37.85%) and Hong Kong (37.57%). According to the latest official statistics on tourist arrivals in Macao, the two largest tourist groups were also from Mainland China and Hong Kong (Macao Statistics and Census Service, 2012c). With regard to occupation and industry, the sample consisted of mainly white-collar workers (25.55%), students (20.19%), and professionals (13.46%); those employed mainly worked in wholesale and retail

Table 1. Demographic Characteristics of Respondents.

	Residents	Tourists	Total
Sex			
Male	166	176	342
Female	197	189	386
Total	363	365	728
Place of residence			
Hong Kong		133	
Mainland China		134	
Thailand		4	
Korea		4	
Taiwan		39	
Japan		5	
Singapore		11	
Malaysia		13	
The Philippines		3	
Others		8	
Industry			
Manufacturing	6	19	25
Electricity, gas, and water supply	4	9	13
Construction	12	15	27
Wholesale and retail	27	50	77
Hotels and restaurants	41	35	76
Transport, storage, and communications	32	33	65
Financial service	26	32	58
Real estate and business activities	16	39	55
Public administration and social security	36	39	75
Gambling	42	4	46
Cultural, arts, and creative	10	15	25
Other	1	0	1
N/A	110	75	185
Age			
15–24	134	72	206
25–34	117	136	253
35–44	60	94	154
45–54	33	59	92
55–64	13	2	15
65 or older	3	0	3
N/A	3	2	5
Education level			
Primary school or below	26	13	39
High school or vocational training	158	133	291
Bachelor's degree or above	168	203	371
N/A	11	16	27
Personal monthly income (US$)			
≤600	95	74	169
601–1,200	53	68	121

(*Continued*)

Table 1. Continued.

	Residents	Tourists	Total
1,201–1,800	89	97	186
1,801–2,400	76	45	121
2,401–3,000	16	32	48
3,001–3,600	4	17	21
>3,600	6	11	17
N/A	24	21	45
Occupation			
Senior management	9	18	27
Professional	39	59	98
White-collar worker	76	110	186
Blue-collar worker	49	39	88
Casino dealer	33	1	34
Students	94	53	147
Unemployed	22	19	41
Self-employed	25	50	75
N/A	16	16	32

Note. Total sample: $N = 728$; Residents: $N = 363$; Tourists: $N = 365$.

(10.58%), hotels and restaurants (10.44%), and public administration and social security (10.3%). Many of the respondents (25.55%) earned an average monthly income of US$1,201–US$1,800. This is very close to the statistics for the population as a whole, with an average median income of around US$1,250 per month (Macao Statistics and Census Service, 2012b). However, an almost equally large portion of the sample (23.21%) were earning equal or less than US$600 per month. These results are tabulated concisely in Table 1.

Results, Analysis, and Discussion

An analysis of the results was undertaken by comparing the frequencies of the observed behaviors cross-referenced with how annoying they were perceived to be. An overview of these behavioral issues is presented through the use of an action grid and then further linking the behaviors to the themed categories identified by the authors, inspired by existing cross-cultural work on the CMM approach—specifically, speech and sound acts, key episodes, relationship interactions, views of the self in relation to society, and broad cultural patterns (Pearce Associates, 1999; B. Pearce, 2005; Philipsen, 1995). Building on these themes, the authors have developed new integrative categories, namely:

1. behaviors directly relating to others;
2. isolated individual acts, which are subdivided into

   a. bodily functions or presentation/appearance issues; and
   b. verbal or sound acts; and

3. marginally illegal or scam behaviors.

Local residents' and tourists' ratings were compared with mean difference testing both individually and categorically. A frequency–annoyance grid was constructed to illustrate the relationship between frequency and annoyance ratings of the behaviors in a neat manner. The data provide a range of key annoying behaviors, some of which are perceived to be relatively frequent.

General Frequency–Annoyance Evaluation

Table 2 presents the frequency–annoyance evaluation of the 40 behavior types by the 728 respondents. Annoyance scores were all higher than frequency scores. Respondents uniformly considered that these behaviors were more annoying than the frequency of encounter. The four most frequently encountered behaviors were, in order from high to low:

1. smoking anywhere without considering those around them,
2. littering/spitting in public,
3. breaking into a line of waiting people, and
4. driving a car or crossing road unsafely/not observing local traffic rules and regulations.

The most annoying behaviors were (a) not flushing the toilet after use, (b) littering/spitting in public, (c) verbally or physically abusing service personnel in hotels and other service operations, and (d) smoking anywhere without considering those around them. These scores are plotted in Figure 1 for a graphic presentation of the distribution along the two-dimensional frequency–annoyance grid. The *x*-axis represents the frequency of encounter and the *y*-axis portrays the level of annoyance associated with these behaviors. The four quadrants were identified and constructed using a scale mean of 2.50 as the cross-hairs for both scales and they were named by borrowing the idea from the importance–performance analysis (IPA) grid often used in the tourism and hospitality literature (Chu & Choi, 2000; Evans & Chon, 1989; Hsu, Byun, & Yang, 1997; Keyt, Yavas, & Riecken, 1994; Lewis & Chambers, 1989; Martin, 1995). The use of this IPA-like grid as one of the ways to present findings is essential to the ready interpretation and readability of the findings. Although various issues related to the use of IPA have been raised, these issues are mainly related to the validity of the attributes of importance and performance but are less concerned with the ability to present data effectively. The grid suggested here resembles IPA in format only because it is considered to be a neat way of presenting results across the frequency and annoyance dimensions. The use of a scale mean (at the level of 2.5 on our 4-point scale) is one of the two main ways of determining the cross-hair points of the grid (Oh, 2001) and has been used by numerous researchers (Evans & Chon, 1989; Hawes & Rao, 1985). The four quadrants identified here are as follows:

- Quadrant I (concentrate here)—behaviors are perceived to be highly annoying and frequently encountered by respondents. These behaviors should be focused on because they will directly affect the emotions of the tourists and hosts.
- Quadrant II (watch out)—behaviors are perceived with high annoyance level but not as frequently seen. Policy makers should continuously watch and observe the trend of these behaviors so that these behaviors will not become more prominent and thus cross over into Quadrant I.
- Quadrant III (let it be)—behaviors are deemed neither annoying nor frequent by the respondents. Policy makers should not preoccupy themselves with these behaviors.

Table 2. Mean Scores of Frequency and Level of Annoyance of Tourist Behavior Types (Whole Sample).

Behavior	Frequency	Level of Annoyance
1. Eating food with a strong smell in a closed environment (e.g., in a bus)	1.71	2.82
2. Breaking into a line of waiting people	2.49	2.89
3. Trying clothes on in public	1.77	2.59
4. Blowing nose loudly in public	2.08	2.62
5. Getting in elevators (or other vehicles) before others get off	2.05	2.69
6. Staring and pointing at people different from themselves	1.94	2.83
7. Disturbing others in public using loud voices	2.25	2.83
8. Being rude to service personnel in hotels and other service operations	1.94	2.77
9. Being overly demanding to service personnel in hotels and other service operations	1.80	2.92
10. Being insensitive to the feeling of service personnel in hotels and other service operations	1.78	2.87
11. Verbally or physically abusing service personnel in hotels and other service operations	1.69	3.13
12. Bumping into others in a crowd	2.32	3.03
13. Grabbing at someone's clothes to get attention or tapping the person's arm	1.86	2.75
14. Smoking anywhere without considering those around them	2.89	3.10
15. Not holding the door for the person behind them	2.06	2.44
16. Gargling noisily after a meal and burping	2.03	2.54
17. Demanding discounts on merchandise at stores	2.22	2.33
18. Slurping loudly while eating soup	1.88	2.49
19. Carrying a large amount of cash for shopping, thus becoming a major target for theft/showing off money or wealth in public	1.82	2.52
20. Littering/spitting in public	2.70	3.19
21. Do not give way/seat to the needy (e.g., elderly, pregnant women, disabled people, etc.)	2.15	2.88
22. Inscribing names on walls or pillars	1.80	2.75
23. Not flushing the toilet after use	2.23	3.23
24. Scratching toes in public	1.90	2.99
25. Taking "souvenirs" from hotels	1.89	2.48
26. Taking photos without permission	2.07	2.41
27. Dressing in an offensive way	1.93	2.47
28. Being too affectionate/sexual in public	2.01	2.42
29. Being drunk in public and causing a disturbance to others	1.81	3.01

(*Continued*)

Table 2. Continued.

Behavior	Frequency	Level of Annoyance
30. Driving a car or crossing the road unsafely/not observing local traffic rules and regulations	2.46	2.84
31. Expecting to be served before locals	1.96	2.85
32. Behaving rudely to other people	2.17	3.01
33. Using foul language such as swearing openly	2.30	3.01
34. Allowing children to go to the toilet in the street	1.89	2.91
35. Lying or sitting on the street in a very casual way	2.23	2.70
36. Participating in criminal activities (e.g., theft and robbery)	1.56	2.98
37. Not respecting the religious or spiritual needs of others	1.69	2.95
38. Not fitting in with the local way of behaving	1.82	2.88
39. Causing congestion or crowding problems by their individual selfishness	2.11	3.00
40. Causing congestion or crowding problems because of their group behaviors	2.06	2.96

- Quadrant IV (low priority)—behaviors are considered to be frequently seen but not very annoying to the respondents. Such behaviors are of no immediate concern or threat to the policy makers and thus limited resources should be extended to this low-priority cell.

In Figure 1, most plots are concentrated and located on the high annoyance range but spread across both high- and low-frequency domains (Quadrant I and Quadrant II), with only a few behaviors falling in the the low annoyance and low-frequency zone (Quadrant III). No behaviors are located in the low-priority zone. For a closer and better view, the framed area is enlarged and reproduced as Figure 2. Figure 2 presents the distribution of the 40 behavior types and five categories and subcategories in the grid (these categories will be discussed later in the section titled "Intergroup Comparison and New Categorical Themes"). All but two behavior types (no. 14, smoking anywhere without considering those around them, and no. 20, littering/spitting in public) and all categories fall in between 1.5 and 2.5 in the low-frequency range. This means that the respondents only found these two behavior types as frequent behaviors, with a few borderline cases, such as no. 2, breaking into a line of waiting people, and no. 30, driving a car or crossing the road unsafely/not observing local traffic rules and regulations. A quick conclusion is that though respondents considered these behaviors mostly annoying, fortunately they were not yet widely prevalent in Macao. There are, however, some cases that deserve more attention. These instances are highlighted by the two intersecting rectangles. These two rectangles identify the top four most annoying and frequently seen behaviors, respectively. The behaviors that call for the most attention are no. 14 and no. 20, namely, smoking anywhere without considering those around them and littering/spitting in public, which fall into the overlapped area. These two behaviors are simultaneously considered to be the most annoying and

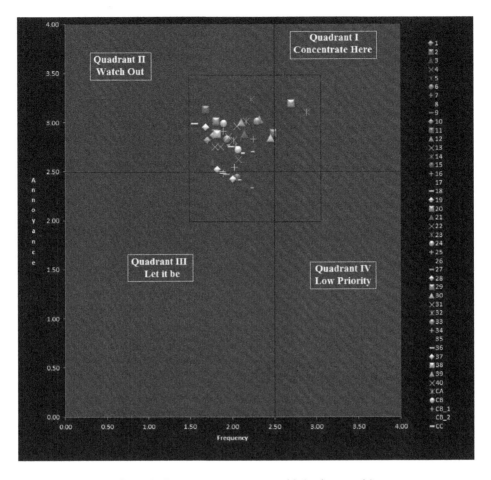

Figure 1. Frequency–annoyance grid (entire sample).

frequent by both residents and tourists. Many articles describing undesirable tourist behaviors have also reported these two behaviors as priority items (BBC News, 2002; Chio, 2010; Nanda, 2008; Zeng, 2006; Zhang, 2006).

Intergroup Comparison and New Categorical Themes

The sections above describe the frequency–annoyance evaluation from a general perspective and include responses from the entire sample. This section investigates intergroup comparison and focuses on any potential (dis)similar views from the two subsample groups, namely, tourists and hosts. This section also organizes the behavior types by the new categorical themes developed by the authors after being inspired by the traditional work of CMM. The development of these new themed categories is due to the inherent ambiguity posited by CMM where there are small specific behaviors embedded in episodes located in relationships framed in life scripts and subsumed within cultural dimensions. In this layered and inclusive conceptual scheme it is sometimes difficult to identify the behaviors as clearly separate in terms of the five levels because they cross over and relate to multiple levels depending on how one has phrased or interpreted them. The

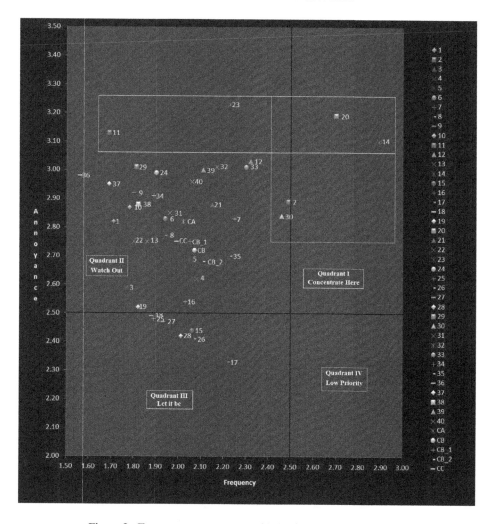

Figure 2. Frequency–annoyance grid (entire sample)—enlarged.

confusion faced by the authors when designing the methodological approach for this study led to the idea of aggregating these tourist behaviors in a new and bold way. The newly developed categories used were as follows: (a) behaviors directly relating to others; (b) isolated individual acts; and (c) marginally illegal or scam behaviors. Category B was further subdivided into bodily functions or presentation/appearance issues and verbal or sound acts to reflect their different nature. The mean scores and *t*-test results between the two groups using these categories as well as the individual elements for the frequency and level of annoyance scores are shown in Table 3.

Frequency and Annoyance Evaluation

Table 3 shows that the mean frequency scores given by the resident group were all higher than those of the tourist group for all 40 behavior types and the differences were significant for 37 of them (except for nos. 15, 25 and 26). These results are not surprising

Table 3. Mean Scores and Intergroup Comparison of Frequency and Level of Annoyance of Tourist Behavior Types.

Behavior Types	Frequency			Level of Annoyance		
	Residents	Tourists	Significance	Residents	Tourists	Significance
Category A: Behaviors directly relating to others (CA)	2.13	1.91	.000**	2.91	2.72	.000**
2. Breaking into a line of waiting people	2.64	2.35	.000**	2.98	2.78	.025*
5. Getting in elevators (or other vehicles) before others get off	2.12	1.97	.018*	2.76	2.62	.074
6. Staring and pointing at people different from themselves	2.01	1.87	.030*	2.93	2.73	.014*
8. Being rude to service personnel in hotels and other service operations	2.06	1.83	.000**	2.86	2.66	.013*
9. Being overly demanding to service personnel in hotels and other service operations	1.95	1.65	.000**	2.97	2.86	.193
10. Being insensitive to the feelings of service personnel in hotels and other service operations	1.89	1.66	.000**	2.94	2.77	.064
11. Verbally or physically abusing service personnel in hotels and other service operations	1.83	1.56	.000**	3.20	3.05	.103
12. Bumping into others in a crowd	2.41	2.24	.011*	3.11	2.94	.012*
13. Grabbing at someone's clothes to get attention or tapping the person's arm	1.93	1.79	.031*	2.85	2.63	.012*
15. Not holding the door for the person behind them	2.12	2.01	.097	2.52	2.35	.031*
21. Do not give way/seat to the needy (e.g., elderly, pregnant women, disabled people, etc.)	2.30	2.00	.000**	2.99	2.75	.001**
32. Behaving rudely to other people	2.34	2.00	.000**	3.08	2.92	.020*
Category B: Isolated individual acts (CB)	2.18	1.96	.000**	2.81	2.62	.000**
Sub-Cat: Bodily functions or presentation/appearance issues (CB_1)	2.16	1.94	.000**	2.84	2.65	.000**
1. Eating food with strong smell in a closed environment (e.g., in a bus)	1.79	1.64	.012*	2.88	2.76	.206
3. Trying clothes on in public	1.86	1.68	.004**	2.66	2.51	.091
14. Smoking anywhere without considering those around them	3.03	2.75	.000**	3.19	3.00	.007**
17. Demanding discounts on merchandise at stores	2.32	2.12	.004**	2.48	2.17	.000**
19. Carrying a large amount of cash for shopping, thus becoming a major target for theft/showing off money or wealth in public	1.88	1.75	.017*	2.65	2.38	.005**

(Continued)

Table 3. Continued.

Behavior Types	Frequency			Level of Annoyance		
	Residents	Tourists	Significance	Residents	Tourists	Significance
23. Not flushing the toilet after use	2.34	2.13	.002**	3.34	3.11	.001**
24. Scratching toes in public	1.97	1.84	.040*	3.08	2.89	.041*
27. Dressing in an offensive way	2.01	1.84	.010**	2.53	2.40	.139
31. Expecting to be served before locals	2.12	1.80	.000**	2.95	2.72	.004**
35. Lying or sitting on the street in a very casual way	2.36	2.10	.000**	2.82	2.56	.002**
38. Not fitting in with the local way of behaving	1.92	1.71	.001**	2.92	2.83	.336
39. Causing congestion or crowding problems by their individual selfishness	2.26	1.96	.000**	2.99	3.01	.804
40. Causing congestion or crowding problems because of their group behaviors	2.21	1.91	.000**	2.91	3.03	.147
Sub-Cat: Verbal or sound acts (CB_2)	2.22	2.00	.000**	2.77	2.58	.000**
4. Blowing nose loudly in public	2.20	1.95	.000**	2.72	2.51	.017*
7. Disturbing others in public using loud voices	2.36	2.13	.001**	2.88	2.76	.089
16. Gargling noisily after a meal and burping	2.15	1.91	.001**	2.61	2.46	.075
18. Slurping loudly while eating soup	1.95	1.81	.034*	2.61	2.36	.014*
33. Using foul language such as swearing openly	2.44	2.17	.000**	3.11	2.90	.004**
Category C: Marginally illegal or scam behaviors (CC)	2.09	1.89	.000**	2.86	2.62	.000**
20. Littering/spitting in public	2.82	2.58	.001**	3.27	3.10	.013*
22. Inscribing names on walls or pillars	1.88	1.72	.015*	2.88	2.61	.003**
25. Taking "souvenirs" from hotels	1.90	1.87	.667	2.62	2.33	.002**
26. Taking photos without permission	2.13	2.01	.077	2.51	2.31	.017*
28. Being too affectionate/sexual in public	2.09	1.93	.018*	2.49	2.34	.075
29. Being drunk in public and causing a disturbance to others	1.94	1.69	.000**	3.14	2.87	.001**
30. Driving a car or crossing the road unsafely/not observing local traffic rules and regulations	2.64	2.29	.000**	2.97	2.70	.001**
34. Allowing children to go to the toilet in the street	2.06	1.72	.000**	2.99	2.79	.031*
36. Participating in criminal activities (e.g., theft and robbery)	1.68	1.43	.000**	3.07	2.85	.039*
37. Not respecting the religious or spiritual needs of others	1.77	1.62	.015*	3.03	2.86	.062

Note. *Significant at the .05 level. **Significant at the .01 level.

because the residents presumably had more frequent contact with the tourists than the tourists themselves. Residents (hosts) who have a longer contact time with tourists experience or encounter both positive and less-than-desirable tourist behaviors and are affected by them more than by tourists who are merely sightseers and whose stays are brief. In the latest report released by the Macao government, the average length of stay of tourists coming to Macao is notably short, only one day, in the third quarter of 2011 (Macao Statistics and Census Service, 2012c). This explains the lower frequency scores recorded for the tourist groups.

Category B behaviors (isolated individual acts) were deemed the most frequently encountered by both the residents and tourists (residents = 2.18, tourists = 1.96). If we consider the subcategories within Category B, then the subset of verbal or sound acts were rated with the highest frequency (residents = 2.22, tourists = 2.00). These results highlight the point that most identified undesirable tourist behaviors were mainly related to individual acts (especially those that cause verbal or sound disturbance) that do not have a direct relationship to (or impact on) others (whether hosts or other tourists). However, the number one most frequently seen behavior (no. 14, smoking anywhere without considering those around them), although classified as an individual act, has an indirect impact on those people in the nearby area (residents = 3.03, tourists = 2.75). In view of this, the Macao government enforced the Regime of Tobacco Prevention and Control on January 1, 2012. "To protect citizens and visitors from exposure to second-hand smoke, smoking is prohibited in most public indoor places such as hospitals, food and beverage establishments, hotels, ports and airports, passenger shelters, shops, museums, karaoke establishments and lifts" (Macao Health Bureau, 2012). Had the survey been conducted after the enforcement of this new regime, the result might have been different.

Though the resident group allocated significantly higher frequency scores to most of the behaviors than the tourists did, opinions regarding the level of annoyance were more closely aligned. Although the mean annoyance scores were generally higher for residents than tourists, except in two behavior types (nos. 39 and 40), the differences were significant for 26 behavior types only (versus 37 in frequency scores). The implication is that although these behaviors were deemed more annoying by residents than the tourists in general, the differences were not as obvious as when reporting frequencies. The two sample groups from different cultural backgrounds showed signs of converging opinions regarding how annoying (or not) these identified behaviors were. This result aligns with the view that the world is becoming more interconnected, with marked cultural differences tending to decrease over time (Dann, 1993; Pizam, 1999a). The most annoying category of behaviors is Category A, behaviors directly relating to others (residents = 2.91, tourists = 2.72), and the single most annoying behavior type was no. 23 (i.e., not flushing toilet after use; residents = 3.34, tourists = 3.11). Respondents unanimously agreed that those behaviors that directly affect others are the most annoying (residents = 2.91, tourists = 2.72). This finding fits well-established explanations of human behaviors using the construct of the degree of personal relevance, a term closely related to an individual's identity or self (Bruner & Postman, 1949; Laverie & Arnett, 2000; Trauer & Ryan, 2005). The general explanation of this perspective is that people are more concerned with (and may accentuate) the impact of topics that are more relevant or closely connected to their personal well-being (cf. Weiner, 2010). The literature on self-serving biases in perception is consistent with this theme and frequently reveals that judgment processes are different when viewing what happens to us and what happens to others (Siegel & Shaughnessy, 1996). In our findings, the respondents might have accentuated the levels of annoyance of the named behaviors that have direct relationship, and thus a higher degree of relevance, to them. In general, both residents and tourists considered most of the identified behaviors as annoying, because most were rated beyond the scale mean of 2.5, indicating an above-average perceived annoyance level toward the majority of the undesirable behaviors. Nevertheless, a relatively positive sign is that these less-than-desirable behaviors are not yet widely prevalent in Macao. Some people (in particular, the hosts) may be increasingly wary of the possible scam behaviors performed by tourists. The results from this study should be able to ease this anxiety somewhat because these behaviors were rated with the lowest frequency scores. We should not, however, underestimate the impact of these less frequent yet annoying behaviors. The cumulative effect of multiple but slightly less frequent annoying behaviors might have its own power because the total effect of these scattered complaints may be irritating but harder to pinpoint and more difficult in the long term to manage due to their diversity.

Conclusion and Relevance

The results reported in this study form a good foundation for the further study of undesirable tourist behaviors. Importantly, this study has set the stage for further work by using an emic approach and developing new themed categories. Additionally, using a pictorial approach to present the frequency and annoyance evaluation for the overall sample offers an easily understood overview of the topic. In the present research the results indicated that most behaviors were validated as being at least mildly annoying, but they extend along the frequency scale from low to high. Smoking in public and spitting and littering were identified as the behaviors that deserve the most immediate attention. Coincidentally, these two behaviors are the most mentioned in popular press articles on problematic tourists.

Tourists and hosts hold quite different perceptions on the overall response patterns, notably in terms of frequency rather than levels of annoyance. Hosts have more frequent encounters with the behaviors than the tourists because hosts reside in the destination and thus have longer exposure to these behaviors. The results also highlight several areas for future attention. Firstly, a majority of behaviors fall into the watch out or concentrate here quadrants in the frequency–annoyance grid, with the two main problematic acts—that of smoking and spitting/littering—being identified as demanding special attention. Although some behaviors are less frequently encountered than others, many are considered annoying. The two big problems are triggers for public discussion, whereas the small annoyances are more cumulative—individually they do not stand out but together they amount to an overall irritation, which can be a problem and should not be overlooked. It should be noted that the frequency of encounters may change over time. These less frequent behaviors may "climb up" the scale and move from the watch out to the concentrate here quadrant as the number of tourist arrivals increases. Macao recorded a 50% increase in tourist arrivals in the years 2004 to 2010 (Macao Statistics and Census Service, 2012d). This upward trend is destined to continue, fueled by the opening of new casinos and integrated entertainment resorts, which promise a further rapid expansion of hotel capacity in Macao. As more tourists come, the impact brought about by these watch out behaviors may become more critical to both tourists and hosts.

The new themed behavioral categories help explain the perceptions of the respondents in a coordinated way. The highest levels of annoyance were associated with behaviors directly affecting others and can be explained by the concept of personal relevance and self-serving biases in attribution. Respondents rated a high level of perceived annoyance for this category due to the fact that these behaviors have direct psychological consequences for them. On the other hand, scam or illegal behaviors are the least frequently encountered and are also rated as less annoying. As previously mentioned, we should not feel contented simply because these behaviors are not yet so frequent. In fact, scattered concerns have been raised by local residents regarding illegal acts suspected to be performed by tourists. Incidences such as stealing stainless steel or iron objects (including the front gates of condominiums and ditch covers) and picking pockets on buses are not unheard of and therefore should be given adequate attention in order to devise precautionary measures before the problems become too big to remedy. Scam behaviors in tourism studies mostly focus on tourists as victims (P. L. Pearce, 2011b). Few studies have attempted to investigate illegal or scam behaviors in which tourists can be offenders themselves. Nonetheless, tourists' participation in illegal or scam acts can cause tension between nations and affect the perceptions of the tourism industry (Lemieux & Felson, 2011).

Drawing from the above points, the potential contributions made by this study are threefold. First, it helps promote better understanding of specific cross-culturally challenging behaviors between tourists and hosts. Furthering mutual understanding is essential for the sustainable development of tourism. Second, it suggests a framework for the typology of problematic tourists. This new framework helps draw meaningful conclusions from a large-scale data set and highlights a way to approach long lists of material. It also identifies the relatively untapped field of inquiry on tourist participation in illegal or scam behaviors. Third, the potential construction of social influence messages and campaigns to limit undesirable behaviors built on these kinds of results may assist in making emerging waves of tourists more globally responsible and well-accepted citizens.

References

Allen, R. L., Long, P. T., Perdue, R., & Kieselbach, S. (1988). The impact of tourism development on residents' perceptions of community life. *Journal of Travel Research*, *27*(1), 16–21.

Argyle, M. (1975). *Bodily communication*. London, England: Methuen.

Arnold, W. (2005, October 21). *Chinese tourists getting a bad image*. Retrieved from http://www.iht.com/bin/print_ipub.php?file=/articles/2005/10/21/business/tourists.php

Ball, P. (2004). *Critical mass: How one thing leads to another*. London, England: Arrow.

BBC News. (2002, July 31). *Who are the world's worst tourists?* Retrieved from http://news.bbc.co.uk/2/hi/talking_point/2138252.stm

Bell, P., Fisher, J., & Loomis, R. (1978). *Environmental psychology*. Philadelphia, PA: W.B. Saunders.

Bitgood, S. (2003). Visitor orientation: When are museums similar to casinos? *Visitor Studies Today*, *6*(1), 10–12.

Bitgood, S. (2006). An analysis of visitor circulation: Movement patterns and the general value principle. *Curator: The Museum Journal*, *49*(4), 463–475.

Blackden, P. (2004). *Holidaymakers from hell—Shocking behaviour by tourists abroad*. London, England: Virgin Books.

Bowen, D., & Clarke, J. (2009). *Contemporary tourist behaviour: Yourself and others as tourists*. Wallingford, England: CABI.

Brown, T. J. (1999). Antecedents of culturally significant tourist behaviour. *Annals of Tourism Research*, *26*(3), 676–700.

Bruner, J. S., & Postman, L. (1949). Perception, cognition, and behavior. *Journal of Personality*, *18*(1), 14–31.

Buhalis, D. (2000). Marketing the competitive destination of the future. *Tourism Management, 21* (1), 97–116.

Business Standard. (2012). *Japanese voted world's best tourists by hoteliers*. Retrieved from http://www.business-standard.com/india/news/japanese-voted-world%5Cs-best-tourists-by-hoteliers/363427/

Caneday, L., & Zeiger, J. (1991). The social, economic, and environmental costs of tourism to gaming community as perceived by its residents. *Journal of Travel Research, 30*(2), 45–49.

Chen, S. C. (2011). *Minimizing dissonance when hosting Mainland Chinese tourists: A model of understanding their role—Clarity and self-efficacy in service delivery*. Paper presented at the 2011 International CHRIE Conference, Denver, CO, July, 2011. Retrieved from http://scholarworks.umass.edu/cgi/viewcontent.cgi?article=1598&context=refereed

China Daily. (2006, September 2). Guidebook spells out etiquette for tourists. Retrieved from http://www.china.org.cn/english/travel/179938.htm

Chio, J. (2010). *China's campaign for civilized tourism: What to do when tourists behave badly*. Retrieved from http://uts.academia.edu/JennyChio/Papers/326020/Chinas_Campaign_for_Civilized_Tourism_What_to_Do_When_Tourists_Behave_Badly

Chu, R. K. S., & Choi, T. (2000). An importance–performance analysis of hotel selection factors in the Hong Kong hotel industry: A comparison of business and leisure travellers. *Tourism Management, 21*(4), 363–377.

Collett, P. (2004). *The book of tells*. London, England: Bantam Books.

Cronen, V. E., & Shuter, R. (1983). Forming intercultural bonds. In W. B. Gudykunst (Ed.), *Intercultural communication theory: Current perspectives* (pp. 89–118). Beverley Hills, CA: Sage.

Dann, G. (1993). Limitations in the use of "nationality" and country of residence variables. In D. Pearce & R. Butler (Eds.), *Tourism research: Critiques and challenges* (pp. 88–112). London, England: Routledge and Kegan Paul.

Dogan, H. Z. (1989). Forms of adjustments: Socio-cultural impacts of tourism. *Annals of Tourism Research, 16*(2), 216–236.

Eibl-Eibesfeldt, I. (1989). *Human ethology*. New York, NY: Aldine de Gruyter.

Evans, M. R., & Chon, K. S. (1989). Formulating and evaluating tourism policy using importance–performance analysis. *Hospitality Education and Research Journal, 13*(1), 203–213.

Falk, J. H., Ballantyne, R., Packer, J., & Benckendorff, P. (2012). Travel and learning: A neglected tourism research area. *Annals of Tourism Research, 39*(2), 908–927.

Goffman, E. (1959). *The presentation of self in everyday life*. New York, NY: Doubleday.

Grossberg, R., Treves, A., & Naughton-Treves, L. (2003). The incidental ecotourist: Measuring visitor impacts on endangered howler monkeys at a Belizean archaeological site. *Environmental Conservation, 30*(1), 40–51.

Hawes, J. M., & Rao, C. P. (1985). Using importance–performance analysis to develop health care marketing strategies. *Journal of Health Care Marketing, 5*(4), 19–25.

Hinde, R. (1972). *Non-verbal communication*. Cambridge, MA: Cambridge University Press.

Hsu, C. H. C., Byun, S., & Yang, I. S. (1997). Attitudes of Korean college students towards quick-service, family-style, and fine dining restaurants. *Journal of Restaurant & Foodservice Marketing, 2*(4), 65–85.

Inskeep, E. (1991). *Tourism planning: An integrated and sustainable development approach*. New York, NY: Van Nostrand Reinhold.

Jacobson, S. K., & Lopez, A. F. (1994). Biological impacts of ecotourism: Tourists and nesting turtles in Tortuguero National Park, Costa Rica. *Wildlife Society Bulletin, 22*(3), 414–419.

Johns, N. (2002). Market segmentation and the prediction of tourist behavior: The case of Bornholm, Denmark. *Journal of Travel Research, 40*(3), 316–327.

Jurowski, C., Uysal, M., & Williams, D. R. (1997). A theoretical analysis of host community residents reactions to tourism. *Journal of Travel Research, 36*(2), 3–11.

Kavallins, I., & Pizam, A. (1994). The environmental impact of tourism—Whose responsibility is it anyway? The case study of Mykonos. *Journal of Travel Research, 33*(2), 26–32.

Keyt, J. C., Yavas, U., & Riecken, G. (1994). Importance–performance analysis: A case study in restaurant positioning. *International Journal of Retail and Distribution Management, 22* (5), 35–40.

Kozak, M., & DeCrop, A. (Eds.). (2009). *Handbook of tourist behaviour: Theory and practice.* New York, NY: Routledge.

Laverie, D. A., & Arnett, D. B. (2000). Factors affecting fan attendance: The influence of identity salience and satisfaction. *Journal of Leisure Research, 32*(2), 225–246.

Lawson, R. W., William, J., Young, T., & Cossens, J. (1998). A comparison of residents' attitudes towards tourism in 10 New Zealand destinations. *Tourism Management, 19*(3), 247–256.

Lemieux, A., & Felson, M. (2011). Tourist and visitor crime. In M. Natarajan (Ed.), *International crime and justice* (pp. 223–228). New York, NY: Cambridge University Press.

Lewis, R. C., & Chambers, R. E. (1989). *Marketing leadership in hospitality.* New York, NY: Van Nostrand Reinhold.

Loukissas, P. (1993). Public participation in community tourism planning: A gaming simulation approach. *Journal of Travel Research, 22*(1), 18–23.

Macao Health Bureau. (2012). *No smoking ordinance now in effect in Macau.* Retrieved from http://portal.gov.mo/web/guest/info_detail?infoid=139164

Macao Statistics and Census Service. (2012a). *2011 Census preliminary results.* Retrieved from http://www.dsec.gov.mo/getAttachment/b6419af3-ba5a-4024-ba3a-3cf172198c9f/ E_CENP_PUB_2011_Y.aspx

Macao Statistics and Census Service. (2012b). *Median monthly earnings of employed population.* Retrieved from http://www.dsec.gov.mo/TimeSeriesDatabase.aspx?lang=en-US&KeyIndicator ID=25

Macao Statistics and Census Service. (2012c). *Principal statistical indicators of Macao—3rd quarter 2011.* Retrieved from http://www.dsec.gov.mo/getAttachment/6e7fa109-2159-4354- b313-ce0ff995ae2e/E_PIEM_FR_2011_Q3.aspx

Macao Statistics and Census Service. (2012d). *Time series data base—Tourism.* Retrieved from http://www.dsec.gov.mo/TimeSeriesDatabase.aspx

Malinowski, B. (2006). *Argonauts of the Western Pacific.* New York, NY: Routledge. (Original work published 1922)

Mansfeld, Y. (1992). Tourism: Towards a behavioural approach: The choice of destination and its impact on spatial behaviour. *Progress in Planning, 38*(1), 1–92.

Maoz, D. (2006). The mutual gaze. *Annals of Tourism Research, 33*(1), 221–239.

Martin, D. W. (1995). An importance–performance analysis of service providers' perception of quality service in the hotel industry. *Journal of Hospitality & Leisure Marketing, 3*(1), 5–17.

Melton, A. W. (1933). Studies of installation at the Pennsylvania Museum of Art. *Museum News, 10*(14), 5–8.

Melton, A. W. (1936). Distribution of attention in galleries in a museum of science and industry. *Museum News, 14*(3), 6–8.

Melton, A. W. (1972). Visitor behavior in museums: Some early research in environmental design. *Human Factors, 14*(5), 393–403.

Milman, A., & Pizam, A. (1988). Socio impacts of tourism on central Florida. *Annals of Tourism Research, 15*(2), 191–204.

Morgan, M., Lugosi, P., & Ritchie, J. R. B. (Eds.). (2010). *The tourism and leisure experience: Consumer and managerial perspectives.* Bristol, England: Channel View.

Morris, D. (1985). *Bodywatching. A field guide to the human species.* London, England: Jonathan Cape.

Morris, M. W., & Mason, M. F. (2009). Intentionality in intuitive versus analytical processing: Insights from social cognitive neuroscience. *Psychological Inquiry, 20*(1), 58–65.

Moscardo, G. (1996). Mindful visitors: Heritage and tourism. *Annals of Tourism Research, 23*(2), 376–397.

Murphy, P. E. (1985). *Tourism: A community approach*. New York, NY: Methuen.

Nanda, S. S. (2008). *Social marketing for national prestige projects—A proposed social change campaign model for the Commonwealth Games 2010*. Retrieved from http://ndc.nic.in/research_papers/Ndc_paper_1_2008.pdf

Oh, H. (2001). Revisiting importance–performance analysis. *Tourism Management, 22*(6), 617–627.

Oppermann, M. (1999). Predicting destination choice—A discussion of destination loyalty. *Journal of Vacation Marketing, 5*(1), 51–65.

Orams, M. B., & Hill, G. J. E. (1998). Controlling the ecotourist in a wild dolphin feeding program: Is education the answer? *Journal of Environmental Education, 29*(3), 33–38.

Payne, D., & Dimanche, F. (1996). Towards a code of conduct for the tourism industry: An ethics model. *Journal of Business Ethics, 15*(9), 997–1007.

Pearce Associates. (1999). *Using CMM, "The coordinated management of meaning."* San Mateo, CA: Author.

Pearce, B. (2005). The coordinated management of meaning (CMM). In W. B. Gudykunst (Ed.), *Theorizing about intercultural communication* (pp. 35–54). Thousand Oaks, CA: Sage Publications.

Pearce, P. L. (1995). From culture shock and culture arrogance to culture exchange: Ideas towards sustainable socio-cultural tourism. *Journal of Sustainable Tourism, 3*(3), 143–154.

Pearce, P. L. (2005). *Tourist behaviour themes and conceptual schemes*. Clevedon, England: Channel View.

Pearce, P. L. (2011a). *Tourist behaviour and the contemporary world*. Bristol, England: Channel View.

Pearce, P. L. (2011b). Tourism scams: Exploring the dimensions of an international tourism phenomenon. *European Journal of Tourism Research, 4*(2), 147–156.

Pearce, P. L., Kim, E., & Lussa, S. (1998). Facilitating tourist host social interaction: An overview and assessment of the Culture Assimilator. In E. Laws, G. Moscardo, & B. Faulkner (Eds.), *Embracing and managing change in tourism: International case studies* (pp. 347–364). London, England: Routledge.

Pearce, P. L., Moscardo, G. M., & Ross, G. F. (1996). *Tourism community relationships*. Oxford, England: Pergamon Press.

Philipsen, G. (1995). The coordinated management of meaning—Theory of Pearce, Cronen and Associates. In D. P. Cushman & B. Kovacic (Eds.), *Watershed research traditions in human communication theory* (pp. 13–44). New York, NY: State University of New York Press.

Pizam, A. (1978). Tourist impacts: The social costs to the destination community as perceived by its residents. *Journal of Travel Research, 16*(1), 8–12.

Pizam, A. (1999a). The American group tourist as viewed by British, Israeli, Korean and Dutch tour guides. *Journal of Travel Research, 38*(2), 119–126.

Pizam, A. (1999b). Cross-cultural tourist behavior. In A. Pizam & Y. Mansfeld (Eds.), *Consumer behavior in travel and tourism* (pp. 393–412). New York, NY: Haworth Press.

Pizam, A., Jansen-Verbeke, M., & Steel, L. (1997). Are all tourists alike regardless of nationality? The perceptions of Dutch tour-guides. *Journal of International Hospitality, Leisure & Tourism Management, 1*(1), 19–40.

Pizam, A., & Mansfeld, Y. (2000). *Consumer behaviour in travel and tourism*. New York, NY: The Haworth Hospitality Press.

Pizam, A., & Sussman, S. (1995). Does nationality affect tourist behavior? *Annals of Tourism Research, 22*(4), 901–917.

Reisinger, Y., & Turner, L. (2003). *Cross-cultural behaviour in tourism*. Oxford, England: Butterworth Heinemann.

Ross, G. F. (1991). A survey of the perceived effects of tourism on older and long-term residents of an Australian city. Unpublished manuscript, James Cook University of North Queensland, Australia.

Ryan, C., Scotland, A., & Montgomery, D. (1998). Resident attitudes to tourism development—A comparative study between the Rangitikei, New Zealand and Bakewell, United Kingdom. *Progress in Tourism and Hospitality Research, 4*(2), 115–130.

Seaton, A. V. (2002). Tourism as metempsychosis and metensomatosis: The personae of eternal recurrence. In G. M. S. Dann (Ed.), *The tourist as a metaphor of the social world* (pp. 135–168). Wallingford, England: CAB International.

Seddighi, H. R., & Theocharous, A. L. (2002). A model of tourism destination choice: A theoretical and empirical analysis. *Tourism Management, 23*(5), 475–487.

Siegel, J., & Shaughnessy, M. F. (1996). An interview with Bernard Weiner. *Educational Psychology Review, 8*(2), 165–174.

Smith, V. L. (1989). *Hosts and guests: The anthropology of tourism* (2nd ed.). Philadelphia, PA: The University of Pennsylvania Press.

Trauer, B., & Ryan, C. (2005). Destination image, romance and place experience—An application of intimacy theory in tourism. *Tourism Management, 26*(4), 481–491.

Ward, C., Bochner, S., & Furnham, A. (2001). *The psychology of culture shock* (2nd ed.). East Sussex, England: Routledge.

Weiner, B. (2010). The development of an attribution-based theory of motivation: A history of ideas. *Educational Psychologist, 45*(1), 28–36.

Zeng, C. (2006, October 5). *Chinese travelers' uncivil liberties.* Retrieved from http://www.atimes.com/atimes/China/HJ05Ad01.html

Zhang, R. (2006, October 8). *Chinese tourists' bad behavior to be curbed.* Retrieved from http://www.china.org.cn/english/2006/Oct/183079.htm

An Empirical Study of Anticipated and Perceived Discrimination of Mainland Chinese Tourists in Hong Kong: The Role of Intercultural Competence

关于中国内地游客在香港的预期和感知歧视的实证研究：跨文化能力的作用

BEN HAOBIN YE
HANQIN QIU ZHANG
PETER P. YUEN

Mainland Chinese tourists constitute the largest portion of tourists in Hong Kong. As such, they are crucial to the tourist industry in Hong Kong. However, some of their dissatisfactory travel experiences do not receive adequate attention from either tourism practitioners or tourism scholars. The current study hopes to fill this research gap through an examination of the factors contributing to both anticipated and perceived discrimination of Mainland Chinese tourists. A questionnaire was distributed to 248 Mainland Chinese tourists in Hong Kong. Multivariate analysis of covariance (MANCOVA) was performed to examine the factors causing variance in anticipated and perceived discrimination. The findings reveal that, when past discriminatory experiences of either self or friends/relatives and the number of visits were controlled for, the intercultural competence of tourists had a significant effect on anticipated and perceived discrimination. Tourists who are more interculturally competent are less likely to anticipate and perceive discrimination. Practical implications are discussed in relation to how to reduce tourists' anticipated and perceived discrimination.

中国内地是香港旅游业最大的客源市场。因此，该市场对香港旅游业的重要性不言而喻。然而，中国内地游客的一些不满意的旅游经历没有受到旅游业界和旅游研究者的足够重视。本研究希望通过探讨影响中国内地游客的预期和感知歧视的因素，以进一步充实该方面的研究。本研究对*248*个在香港旅行的内地游客进行问卷调查。所收数据通过*MANCOVA*分析，探讨影响预期和感知歧视的因素。结果表明，当游客自身及其亲戚朋友过往的歧视经历，以及游客到访香港的次数这几个变量被控制后，游客的跨文化能力对其预期和感知歧视有显著

Ben Haobin Ye is Lecturer in the School of Business at Sun Yat-sen University, Guangzhou, China.

Hanqin Qiu Zhang is Associate Professor in the School of Hotel and Tourism Management at The Hong Kong Polytechnic University, Kowloon, Hong Kong, China.

Peter P. Yuen is Professor and Dean of The College of Professional and Continuing Education at The Hong Kong Polytechnic University, Kowloon, Hong Kong, China.

影响。跨文化能力越高的游客，其预期和感知歧视越小。同时文章也讨论了如何减少游客预期和感知歧视。

关键词: 中国内地游客，感知歧视，跨文化能力，香港

Introduction

Mainland Chinese tourists constitute the largest portion of tourists in Hong Kong. In 2010, this market segment comprised more than 60% of total tourists (Hong Kong Tourism Board, 2011). Extant research has been conducted to examine Mainland Chinese tourists' motivations, behaviors, and experiences in Hong Kong (Choi, Liu, Pang, & Chow, 2008; Huang & Hsu, 2005; Law, To, & Goh, 2008; Zhang & Lam, 1999). However, their dissatisfactory travel experiences have not received adequate scholarly attention.

In recent years, there have been a growing number of incidents between Hongkongers and Mainland Chinese involving conflict, prejudice, and discrimination (Wan, 2012). Mainland Chinese tourists have been accused of violating social rules and norms (e.g., eating on the train) and causing a series of social problems (e.g., pushing up the prices of consumer goods and property; Chow, 2012). On the other side, some Chinese tourists have felt that they do not receive proper treatment from Hongkongers during their visits. For example, Huang and Hsu (2005) found that quite a number of Mainland Chinese tourists expressed disappointment at Hongkongers' display of superiority over them. Ye, Zhang, and Yuen (in press) revealed that both general tourists and medical tourists in Hong Kong experienced different types of unfair treatments (e.g., less respect and courtesy), some of which were attributed to discrimination.

Recently, a dispute between a Hong Kong local and a Mainland Chinese tourist who was caught eating on the metro triggered a widespread debate between Hongkongers and Mainlanders (Chow, 2012). Some Hongkongers took out an advertisement in a local newspaper, describing Mainlanders as locusts (Wan, 2012). Chinese tourists have been accused of violating the social rules in Hong Kong, and some Chinese counterparts claim that they are experiencing discrimination.

The interactions between hosts and tourists have been well documented in the tourism literature (Pearce, 1982; Reisinger & Turner, 2002; Wei, Crompton, & Reid, 1989). Tourists and hosts who have different cultural backgrounds inevitably engage in cross-cultural interactions. Reisinger and Turner (2002) argued that the cultural differences in values, rules of social behavior, perceptions, and social interactions may potentially influence host–tourist interactions. To address the determinants of the outcomes of cross-cultural interaction, the concept of *intercultural competence* was introduced. It refers to people's ability to think and act in appropriate ways with people from other cultures (Friedman & Antal, 2005). People who have high intercultural competence will overcome the cultural constraints and generate appropriate strategies for intercultural interactions (Friedman & Antal, 2005). Nevertheless, the role of intercultural competence in the cross-cultural interactions between tourists and hosts has been underresearched by tourism scholars.

Prior research suggests that some tourists may anticipate discrimination before the actual service encounter (Ye et al., in press), and it is likely that such anticipation may lead to tourists' perceived discrimination because tourists may adjust their perceptions of service toward their prior expectations according to the assimilation theory (Sherif & Hovland, 1961). In view of the above, the current study aims to first investigate correlates of anticipated and perceived discrimination of Mainland Chinese tourists and, second, examine the effect of intercultural competence on both anticipated and perceived discrimination of Mainland Chinese tourists.

The current study serves as one of the pioneer empirical studies to examine perceived discrimination of tourists using an intercultural perspective. The research also sheds light on correlates of tourists' perceived discrimination. The discrimination that Mainland Chinese tourists perceive will have a detrimental effect on the image of Hong Kong as a desirable tourist destination. The current research offers practical solutions for both the government and service providers to minimize discrimination against tourists from Mainland China.

Literature Review

Research on Discrimination

Discrimination consists of negative behaviors, which includes avoidance, active exclusion, and physical attack, toward individuals based on their group membership (e.g., race, ethnicity; Allport, 1954; Taylor, Peplau, & Sears, 2006). Previous studies have suggested that group identification, differences in relative group status, prototypical events, and salient characteristics of cultural identity can affect perceived discrimination (Bettencourt, Charlton, Dorr, & Hume, 2001; Major & Sawyer, 2009; Sellers & Shelton, 2003; Smart & Smart, 1995). Ethnic group members who express a strong group identification are more likely to make an attribution to discrimination (Major, Quinton, & Schmader, 2003). Prototypical events, such as when a Black person receives negative feedback from a White person, enhance the attribution to discrimination by the Black person. Smart and Smart (1995) also demonstrated that language barriers, differences in skin color, and salient ethnic and cultural differences increase the likelihood of discrimination.

Discrimination in the Marketplace

Marketplace discrimination has been referred to as the differential treatment of customers in the marketplace based on perceived group-level traits that produce outcomes favorable to in-groups and unfavorable to out-groups (Crockett, Grier, & Williams, 2003). Discrimination is any unfair treatment that is based on group membership (Major et al., 2002). Prior studies have reported marketplace discrimination in retail and health care settings, which have consisted of incidents of racial discrimination as well as discrimination against obese customers (Baker, Meyer, & Johnson, 2008; Crockett et al., 2003; King & Shapiro, 2006).

There are a limited number of studies in the tourism literature examining the perceived discrimination of tourists (Philipp, 1994; Willming, 2001). In one such study, it was demonstrated that some college-educated African Americans perceived racial discrimination while using travel services and engaging in various tourist activities (Willming, 2001). The study also revealed that demographic variables and perceived racial discrimination collectively explain differences in the travel behaviors of African Americans. Similarly, Philipp (1994) argued that racial prejudice and discrimination may explain differences in the travel preferences of Black and White people in the United States. These studies emphasize the impacts of perceived discrimination on people's travel behaviors. However, not much scholarly work has focused on understanding the formation of perceived discrimination and its antecedents. Ye et al. (in press) conducted a number of in-depth interviews with tourists and found that four groups of factors contribute to tourists' perceived discrimination: tourist factors, cultural factors, employee factors, and contextual factors. Nevertheless, the proposed relationships have not been examined using quantitative methodologies.

In the marketing literature, only a limited number of studies have examined the antecedents of discrimination. Walsh (2009) argued that an employee's demographics and firm-level determinants (e.g., customer orientation) constituted the antecedents of perceived discrimination. Although these factors offer insights into perceived discrimination, they focus solely on service providers, which is only one side of the customer–employee dyad. Moreover, these factors are derived from the literature and have not been tested empirically.

Anticipated Discrimination and Perceived Discrimination

Compared to the research on perceived discrimination, the number of studies on anticipated discrimination is few. Prior research suggests that anticipated discrimination could be formed before any occurrences of actual discrimination. For example, in the psychiatric literature, one study demonstrated that many people who have a mental illness will anticipate discrimination even when no discrimination was experienced (Thornicroft, Brohan, Rose, Sartorius, & Leese, 2009). In addition, it was revealed that anticipated discrimination and experienced discrimination were positively correlated. Prior research also indicates that Chinese tourists who have experienced discrimination in the past may anticipate discrimination before their actual visit to Hong Kong (Ye et al., in press). Hence, it is necessary to examine tourists' anticipated discrimination as it may relate to perceived discrimination as inferred from the assimilation theory (Sherif & Hovland, 1961). In the current study, *anticipated discrimination* is defined as a tourist's anticipation of service providers' differential treatment based on their group membership.

Cross-Cultural Interaction and Intercultural Competence

It is argued that cultural distance may form the basis of prejudice and discrimination. Pearce (1982) claimed that difficulties in interactions due to large cultural differences are important factors in understanding negative host reactions to tourists. Reisinger and Turner (2002) argued that cultural factors are most influential in determining the outcome of intercultural contact between hosts and guests. Ye at al. (in press) found that cultural differences in social norms contribute to perceived discrimination of Mainland Chinese tourists in Hong Kong. However, they also noted that tourists who are more interculturally competent (e.g., can speak the local language) are less likely to perceive discrimination despite cultural differences (Ye et al., in press). People who are interculturally competent will overcome the constraints embedded in one's culturally shaped practices and value systems and generate appropriate strategies for intercultural interactions (Friedman & Antal, 2005). Hence, it is important to investigate how the intercultural competence of tourists affects their perceived discrimination.

Intercultural competence and other similar concepts (e.g., intercultural sensitivity) have been receiving increasing attention in the social psychology literature (Bennett, 1986; Friedman & Antal, 2005; Gibson & Zhong, 2005; Spencer-Rodgers & McGovern, 2002). *Intercultural competence* refers to the ability to think and act in appropriate ways with people from other cultures (Friedman & Antal, 2005) and has been classified into six competencies: language competence, adaption, social decentering, communication effectiveness, social integration, and knowledge of the host culture (Redmond, 2000).

Intercultural competence varies among and can be developed in individuals. One antecedent of intercultural competence is past intercultural experience (Gibson & Zhong, 2005). Bennett (1986) identified six stages of coping with a different culture:

1. denial of difference;
2. defense;
3. minimization;
4. acceptance;
5. adaptation; and
6. integration.

It is argued that tourists are more likely to stay in the denial or defense stage when there are limited opportunities for interaction with the host population (Sharma, Tam, & Kim, 2009).

The number of times that tourists visit a destination may affect their intercultural competence as well. When tourists experience a different culture for the first time, they have to confront cultural differences in areas such as customs, values, service standards, and expectations, which can lead to discomfort (Reisinger & Turner, 2003). After paying multiple visits to the same destination, some tourists gradually acquire knowledge of the host culture. They learn some of the local language, can interpret behaviors, and know what to expect from the host, and they discover appropriate ways to interact. Therefore, their intercultural competence is enhanced by actively engaging with cultural differences through adaptation and integration (Friedman & Antal, 2005). After accumulating travel experience in one particular destination, some tourists will be more capable of adapting their beliefs and behaviors to the host culture. Other tourists will be less likely to do so if they are unwilling or have weak cognitive ability in learning and adapting to a different culture.

It is expected that tourists who have higher intercultural competence are less likely to anticipate and perceive discrimination based on the following reasons. They may have a better understanding of the local language and rules of social behavior and thus are less likely to anticipate discrimination (e.g., sharing less information) arising from potential communication difficulties and violation of norms during service encounters. They are more confident in overcoming intercultural barriers such as language, social norms, and rules. Similarly, those tourists may be less likely to perceive discrimination because they are more skilled in dealing with others who are culturally different, resulting in fewer problems in cross-cultural interaction. Prior research also suggests that ethnic minorities who have high intergroup competence are less likely to perceive discrimination (Phinney, Madden, & Santos, 1998).

The service quality of organized tours has been a burning issue in the tourism industry in Hong Kong. As a usual practice, many tour groups are directed to some designated shopping venues (e.g., jewelry, electronics shops, etc.) and some are required to purchase a certain amount of goods. It was reported that some tourists allegedly received poorer treatment if the expected consumption was not met (Ngo & Nip, 2011). Recently, there have been a number of incidents pertaining to disputes between Chinese tourists and tour guides (Cheung, 2011; Ho, 2011). Hence, those who join a tour (especially a low-fee tour) may anticipate that they will receive poorer services if their intended consumption does not meet the amount expected by the tour guide. Similarly, those who do not purchase enough goods are more likely to perceive discrimination. This perception may be more easily formed by tourists who join tours because they have more chances to detect differential treatment through communication with other group members. Based on the literature review, the following hypotheses were developed:

H1: Mainland Chinese tourists' intercultural competence and travel arrangements have a significant influence on their anticipated and perceived discrimination, such that:

H1a: Mainland Chinese tourists who are more interculturally competent, compared to those who are less competent, have lower levels of anticipated and perceived discrimination.

H1b: Mainland Chinese tourists who join tours, compared to those who make their own travel arrangements, will have a higher level of anticipated discrimination and perceived discrimination.

Methodology

A survey was conducted with 248 tourists from Mainland China in Hong Kong. Convenience sampling was adopted due to the lack of a sampling frame. Intercept surveys were conducted at the Avenue of Stars (the second most visited attraction in Hong Kong), other public leisure areas in Tsim Sha Tsui, and a long-haul bus station where many Mainland Chinese tourists assemble. The data collection period lasted 2 months. To avoid social desirability bias, the questionnaires were self-administered. The order of items was counterbalanced to minimize common method bias. The demographics of the sample (e.g., gender, age, origins, etc.) are quite consistent with the data provided by the Hong Kong Tourism Board (Hong Kong Tourism Board, 2011).

Existing scales were adapted to measure the constructs in the study. The items for intercultural competence were adapted from the Sociocultural Adaptation Scale (SCAS) developed by Ward and Kennedy (1999). The scale was originally used to measure the behavioral components of intercultural competence. In addition to the behavioral dimension, a recent study captured the cognitive aspect of intercultural competence (Friedman & Antal, 2005). Six items from the SCAS were adapted for the study. For example, respondents were required to indicate their difficulties in "adapting to local etiquette," ranging from 1 (*extreme difficulty*) to 5 (*no difficulty*). The measurement of perceived discrimination was adapted from Sandhu and Asrabadi (1994) and Barnes et al. (2004). Five items were used to measure differential treatment in the marketplace. Each item was rated on a 7-point Likert-type scale ranging from 1 (*strongly disagree*) to 7 (*strongly agree*). Past experiences and anticipated discrimination were measured using scales similar to that used for perceived discrimination with some minor changes. For example in responding to the statement "I anticipate that I would be treated with less courtesy than other customers," respondents were asked to recall their anticipation prior to their visit to Hong Kong. Although this might result in retrospective bias, this recall method has been accepted in the tourism field to measure respondents' expectations (Bosque & Martín 2008). In addition, respondents only needed to recall their anticipation from a few days before the interview. Hence, retrospective bias was not a major concern. A back-to-back translation technique was used to minimize translation bias.

Results

Characteristics of Respondents

Table 1 summarizes the demographics of survey respondents. There were slightly more female respondents (54%) than male (46%). The majority of the Chinese respondents were younger than 46 years old (85.1%). There were more married respondents than single and divorced. In general, the respondents' occupations were quite evenly distributed among business sectors, with more respondents who are technicians/engineers (16.1%) and managers/administrators (12.9%) than other occupations. The majority of the respondents (over 80%) had a college-level or above education. Over two thirds of the respondents had a monthly personal income of less than US$1,000. Slightly more than half of the respondents were first-time visitors to Hong Kong. Nearly one quarter of respondents had made multiple visits to Hong Kong. Nearly 40% of the Mainland Chinese tourists were interviewed on the first day and 35% on the second day of their visits. Slightly more Chinese tourists made their own travel arrangements (54%) compared to those who joined tours (see Table 1).

Table 1. Characteristics of Respondents.

	Number	Percentage
Gender		
Male	114	46.0
Female	134	54.0
Age		
16–25	68	27.4
26–35	90	36.3
36–45	53	21.4
46–55	26	10.5
56–65	7	2.8
Over 65	4	1.6
Marital status		
Married	138	55.6
Single	106	42.7
Divorced	4	1.6
Occupation		
Government official	16	6.5
Professor/teacher/researcher	18	7.3
Manager/administrator	32	12.9
Private businessman/woman	22	8.9
Technician/engineer	40	16.1
Office clerk	32	12.9
Factory worker	9	3.6
Self-employed	7	2.8
Student	19	7.7
Retired	12	4.8
Other	41	16.5

(Continued)

Table 1. Continued.

	Number	Percentage
Education		
Postgraduate	25	10.1
College/university	175	70.6
Secondary/high school	46	18.5
Primary/elementary school	2	0.8
No formal education	0	0
Monthly income (US$)		
Less than 500	86	34.7
501–1,000	79	31.9
1,001–2,000	56	22.6
2,001–3,000	15	6.0
3,001–4,000	4	1.6
4,001–5,000	2	0.8
5,001–7,000	2	0.8
7,001–8,000	3	1.2
More than 8,000	1	0.4
Number of visits		
First time	135	54.4
Second time	42	16.9
More than 2	71	28.6
Number of days in Hong Kong prior to survey		
First day	100	40.3
Second day	87	35.1
More than 2	61	24.6
Travel arrangement		
Tour	114	46.0
Made one's own travel plans	134	54.0

Note. N = 248.

Descriptive Statistics and Reliability

The data measuring perceived discrimination, which is the focus of the study, are worthy of discussion. The mean of all measurement variables was below 3, suggesting that perceived discrimination among Mainland Chinese tourists is low in Hong Kong. However, the standard deviation and the maximum value of each variable indicate that some tourists did perceive discrimination. The histograms of these variables show that there were some values higher than 4 (i.e., neutral), confirming the presence of perceived discrimination. Similarly, anticipated discrimination of tourists exists, although the mean scores were relatively low. The intercultural competence of respondents was somewhat high, though there was some variance within the sample. The descriptive statistics are shown in Table 2. All scales reached an acceptable level of 0.70. Exploratory factor analysis was applied to examine the dimensionality of the constructs. Specifically, principle component analysis with varimax rotation was performed. The final scale of each construct in the study exhibited unidimensionality, and the factor loadings for each item were all above the acceptable level of 0.4 (Hair, Black, Babin, & Anderson, 2010).

Table 2. Descriptive Statistics and Reliability.

Construct	Mean	Standard Deviation	Cronbach's α
Perceived discrimination	2.67	1.07	0.85
Anticipated discrimination	2.44	0.97	0.90
Intercultural competence	4.10[a]	0.76	0.78
Past discriminatory experience (self)	1.79	1.17	0.96
Past discriminatory experience (friends and relatives)	2.08	1.16	0.96

Note. [a]Based on a 5-point Likert scale. All others were 7-point scales.

Grouping

The respondents were classified into two groups according to the mean score of their intercultural competence (IC). One hundred eight tourists had low IC (i.e., lower than the mean score) and 140 had high IC (i.e., higher than the mean score). Ninety-three tourists were part of a tour, and 155 tourists had made their own travel arrangements. Perceived discrimination and anticipated discrimination were highly correlated ($r = 0.50, p < .01$) and were thus eligible to be dependent variables in multivariate analysis of covariance (MANCOVA). MANCOVA was performed to test the hypotheses. Intercultural competence, types of travel arrangements, and their interaction were treated as predictors of anticipated discrimination and perceived discrimination. As discussed in the Literature Review section, tourists' intercultural competence is enhanced after multiple visits to a destination; thus, the number of visits should be controlled for in the analysis. As tourists' past discriminatory experiences (theirs and those of their friends) and the number of visits to Hong Kong may impact anticipated and perceived discrimination; these factors were treated as covariates in the MANCOVA.

MANCOVA

The results shown in Table 3 reveal that both past personal discriminatory experiences, $F(2,240) = 10.93, p < .01$, and those of their friends, $F(2,240) = 9.93, p < .01$, as well as the number of visits, $F(2,240) = 6.40, p < .01$, were significant predictors. The interaction effect between intercultural competence and type of travel arrangements was not significant, $F(2,240) = 1.67$. The main effect of intercultural competence, $F(2,240) = 5.43, p < .01$, was highly significant; the effect of the type of travel arrangement, $F(2,240) = 1.81$, was not significant. In particular, Mainland Chinese tourists who had a higher level of intercultural competence reported a lower level of anticipated discrimination (M_{high} IC = 2.28 vs. M_{low} IC = 2.66) and perceived discrimination (M_{high} IC = 2.53 vs. M_{low} IC = 2.86) than those who had a lower level of intercultural competence. Although those who made their own travel arrangements reported a lower level of anticipated discrimination (M_{own} = 2.39 vs. M_{tour} = 2.53) and perceived discrimination (M_{own} = 2.59 vs. M_{tour} = 2.82) than those who joined tours, the difference was not significant.

Table 3. MANCOVA Results.

Variables	Pillai's Trace	F	df	Error df
Perceived discriminatory experience (self)	0.083	10.93*	2	240
Perceived discriminatory experience (friends and relatives)	0.076	9.93*	2	240
Number of visits	0.051	6.40*	2	240
Travel arrangements	0.015	1.81	2	240
Intercultural competence	0.043	5.43*	2	240
Travel Arrangement × Intercultural Competence	0.014	1.67	2	240

Note. *$p < .01$.

Discussion

The findings suggest that tourists who are more interculturally competent are less likely to anticipate and perceive discrimination. Hence, H1a is supported. On the one hand, Chinese tourists who have a better understanding of the social norms of Hong Kong may more easily adapt their behaviors to the local norms and thus are less likely to encounter conflicts between the host population and themselves. On the other hand, as found in our results, 38.7% of the respondents chose "no difficulty" in "understanding the local language." Those Chinese tourists who had greater competence in the local language were able to communicate with the Hong Kong service providers more efficiently, resulting in fewer communication problems that can lead to perceived discrimination. Not surprisingly, the number of visits also had a significant effect on anticipated and perceived discrimination because tourists' intercultural competence was enhanced after multiple visits to Hong Kong.

Although Hong Kong and China share common cultural roots, the former has been Westernized to some extent because it was a colony of the United Kingdom for more than a century. Prior research has revealed the perceived cultural differences between Mainland Chinese and Hong Kong Chinese as they relate to this history (Hong, Chiu, Yeung, & Tong, 1999). Hong Kong Chinese view themselves as more Westernized along several dimensions (e.g., democratic beliefs, social conscientiousness) and distinctive from their Mainland counterparts. Mainland Chinese also believe that Hong Kong Chinese are more Westernized in terms of self-direction, universalism, stimulation, and achievement (Lai, 1998). Further research shows that such value incongruence results in Mainland Chinese's negative attitudes toward Hongkongers (Guan et al., 2009, 2011). Nevertheless, tourists' intercultural competence may overcome such cultural barriers because tourists with high intercultural competence should be able to, to some extent, think and act like Hongkongers. For example, those tourists may understand what kinds of behaviors are socially accepted and not accepted. Hence, mutual understanding may be enhanced, resulting in a decrease in unfavorable outcomes (e.g., discrimination).

The type of travel arrangements did not have a significant effect on Chinese tourists' anticipated and perceived discrimination. In other words, there was no significant difference in terms of anticipated and perceived discrimination between Chinese tourists who joined tours and those who made their own travel arrangements. Thus, H1b is not supported. Future research should examine the nature of the tour (low-fee tour versus high-fee tour). When tour fees are too low and tour groups cannot provide tour guides, whose main income is from commissions on purchases made by tourists, with reasonable remuneration, differential treatment from the tour guides may be more likely to occur.

Past discriminatory experiences of tourists and their friends had a significant influence on anticipated and perceived discrimination. First, the results were consistent with prior research suggesting that past experience is an important antecedent to service expectation (Bolton & Drew, 1991; Zeithaml, Berry, & Parasuraman, 1993). Tourists who have had past discriminatory experiences are more likely to anticipate discrimination, and such anticipation may also result in perceived discrimination. Assimilation theory (Sherif & Hovland, 1961) proposes that people may adjust their perceptions to meet their prior expectations. In the current study, Chinese tourists who had anticipated discrimination might adjust their perceptions of service toward their prior anticipation. In sum, the effect of past discriminatory experiences on anticipated and perceived discrimination is in line with prior research.

Conclusion and Implications

The current research serves as a pioneer study that demonstrates that tourists' intercultural competence can reduce their anticipated and perceived discrimination. In particular, Mainland Chinese tourists who had relatively high intercultural competence were less prone to anticipate and perceive discrimination. In addition, tourists who reported fewer past discriminatory experiences (by both themselves and their friends) and those who had visited Hong Kong several times anticipated and perceived discrimination significantly less.

Although the concept of intercultural competence has been investigated in the literature on cross-cultural interactions, little effort has been made to add to the tourism literature by exploring this concept in relation to tourists' travel experiences. The current study fills this research gap by demonstrating the effects of tourists' intercultural competence on their anticipated and perceived discrimination. Future research on tourist behavior may consider incorporating intercultural competence to enhance the predictive power of the behavioral model.

The tourism industry will continue to play an important role in the economy of Hong Kong. The results of this empirical study have implications for the government and the tourism industry in their formulation of effective policies and measures. The government may help Mainland Chinese tourists enhance their intercultural competence so that they can more easily adapt to the local culture. It is noted that some notices concerning social rules in the metro were written in local oral languages that Mainland Chinese may not understand. In view of this, it might be beneficial if the government could communicate Hong Kong's local rules and norms in a way that is more familiar and comfortable for Mainland Chinese tourists. Enhancement of Mainland Chinese tourists' intercultural competence can reduce the conflicts and problems that they may encounter during their travels in Hong Kong.

If the government has a greater understanding of the current situation, it can implement measures to prohibit discrimination against tourists. In Hong Kong, discrimination is legally prohibited. The Basic Law (Article 39 of the Basic Law) and the Hong Kong Bill of Rights Ordinance (Article 22 of the Hong Kong Bill of Rights Ordinance) prohibit racial discrimination by the government and public authorities. The Race Discrimination Ordinance, passed in 2008 and enacted in 2009, extends the prohibition of race discrimination into the private sector (e.g., goods and services provision; Equal Opportunities Commission, 2008). Despite the enactment of discrimination legislation, Mainland Chinese tourists are not protected by the anti-racism laws mentioned above because they are of the same race. From a policy point of view, the government should consider adding measures to the current anti-discrimination laws to enlarge the protective umbrella covering people from Mainland China. Tourism practitioners should enhance the training of service employees to ensure that equitable and quality service can be delivered to all customers.

Although this study sheds light on the perceived discrimination of Mainland Chinese tourists in Hong Kong, it is not without limitations. First, the study is one-sided in nature, focusing only on tourists. Future research should study service providers as well to elucidate the underlying reasons for perceived discrimination. Second, although the sample characteristics were quite consistent with the data from the Hong Kong Tourism Board (Hong Kong Tourism Board, 2011), the findings may not be generalizable to all Mainland Chinese tourists in Hong Kong due to the use of convenience sampling.

Future research could take many productive directions. First, research can be conducted with tourists and service employees to examine the impact of intercultural competence on both groups of people. Second, a pre- and postvisit measure of independent variables and dependent variables should be taken. Third, a study of other variables as correlates of anticipated and perceived discrimination (e.g., cultural value) is recommended.

References

Allport, G. W. (1954). *The nature of prejudice*. Cambridge, MA: Addison Wesley.

Article 39 of the Basic Law. (2008). The Basic Law of the Hong Kong Special Administrative Region of the People's Republic of China, Constitutional and Mainland Affairs Bureau, pp. 21–22.

Article 22 of the Hong Kong Bill of Rights Ordinance. Retrieved 29 Oct. 2012 from http://www.hklii.hk/eng/hk/legis/ord/383/

Baker, T. L., Meyer, T., & Johnson, J. D. (2008). Individual differences in perceptions of service failure and recovery: The role of race and discriminatory bias. *Journal of the Academy of Marketing Science, 36*(4), 552–564.

Barnes, L. L., De Leon, C. F. M., Wilson, R. S., Bienias, J. L., Bennett, D. A., & Evans, D. A. (2004). Racial differences in perceived discrimination in a community population of older Blacks and Whites. *Journal of Aging and Health, 16*(3), 315–337.

Bennett, M. J. (1986). Towards ethnorelativism: A developmental model of intercultural sensitivity. In R. M. Paige (Ed.), *Cross-cultural orientation: New conceptualizations and applications* (pp. 27–70). New York, NY: University Press of America.

Bettencourt, B. A., Charlton, K., Dorr, N., & Hume, D. L. (2001). Status differences and ingroup bias: A meta-analytic examination of the effects of status stability, status legitimacy, and group permeability. *Psychological Bulletin, 127*(4), 520–542.

Bolton, R. N., & Drew, J. H. (1991). A multistage model of customers' assessments of service quality and value. *Journal of Consumer Research, 17*(4), 375–384.

Bosque, I. R., & Martín, H. S. (2008). Tourist satisfaction: A cognitive–affective model. *Annals of Tourism Research, 35*(2), 551–573.

Cheung, S. (2011, October 7). Tour guide assault charges dropped. *South China Morning Post*, City 4.

Choi, T. M., Liu, S. C., Pang, K. M., & Chow, P. S. (2008). Shopping behaviors of individual tourists from the Chinese Mainland to Hong Kong. *Tourism Management, 29*(4), 811–820.

Chow, V. (2012, February 1). Anger at Mainland visitors escalates with "locust" ad. *South China Morning Post*, City 1.

Crockett, D., Grier, S. A., & Williams, J. A. (2003). Coping with marketplace discrimination: An exploration of the experiences of Black men. *Academy of Marketing Science Review, 4*, 1–18.

Equal Opportunities Commission. (2008). *Race discrimination ordinance and I.* Retrieved from http://www.eoc.org.hk/eoc/GraphicsFolder/showcontent.aspx?content=Race%20Discrimination%20Ordinance%20And%20I

Friedman, V. J., & Antal, A. B. (2005). Negotiating reality: A theory of action approach to intercultural competence. *Management Learning, 36*(1), 69–86.

Gibson, D., & Zhong, M. (2005). Intercultural communication competence in the healthcare context. *International Journal of Intercultural Relations, 29*(5), 621–634.

Guan, Y., Bond, M. H., Huang, Z., Zhang, Z., Deng, H., Hu, T., & Gao, H. (2009). Role of personal endorsement of outgroup members' distinctive values and need for cognitive closure in attitude towards the outgroup. *Asian Journal of Social Psychology, 12*(1), 54–62.

Guan, Y., Verkuyten, M., Fung, H. H., Bond, M. H., Chen, S., & Chan, C. C. (2011). Out-group value incongruence and intergroup attitude: The roles of common identity and multiculturalism. *International Journal of Intercultural Relations, 35*(3), 377–385.

Hair, J. F., Black, W. C., Babin, B. J., & Anderson, R. E. (2010). *Multivariate data analysis.* Upper Saddle River, NJ: Pearson.

Ho, S. (2011, February 18). The ugly tourists. *The Standard*, pp. 18–19.

Hong Kong Tourism Board. (2011). *Visitor arrival statistics.* Hong Kong, China.

Hong, Y. Y., Chiu, C. Y., Yeung, G., & Tong, Y. (1999). Effects of self-categorization on intergroup perceptions: The case of Hong Kong facing 1997. *International Journal of Intercultural Relations, 23*(2), 257–279.

Huang, S., & Hsu, C. H. C. (2005). Mainland Chinese residents' perceptions and motivations of visiting Hong Kong: Evidence from focus group interviews. *Asia Pacific Journal of Tourism Research, 10*(2), 191–205.

King, E. B., & Shapiro, J. R. (2006). The stigma of obesity in customer service: A mechanism for remediation and bottom-line consequences of interpersonal discrimination. *Journal of Applied Psychology, 91*(3), 579–593.

Lai, M. (1998). *Under the two systems: Comparing the ethnic stereotypes and identification patterns of Hong Kong and Guangzhou people* (Unpublished master's thesis). Chinese University of Hong Kong, Hong Kong, China.

Law, R., To, T., & Goh, C. (2008). How do Mainland Chinese travelers choose restaurants in Hong Kong? An exploratory study of individual visit scheme travelers and packaged travelers. *International Journal of Hospitality Management, 27*(3), 346–354.

Major, B., Gramzow, R. H., McCoy, S. K., Levin, S., Schmader, T., & Sidanius, J. (2002). Perceiving personal discrimination: The role of group status and legitimizing ideology. *Journal of Personality and Social Psychology, 82*(3), 269–282.

Major, B., Quinton, W. J., & Schmader, T. (2003). Attributions to discrimination and self-esteem: Impact of group identification and situational ambiguity. *Journal of Experimental Social Psychology, 39*(3), 220–231.

Major, B., & Sawyer, P. J. (2009). Attributions to discrimination: Antecedents and consequences. In T. D. Nelson (Ed.), *Handbook of prejudice, stereotyping, and discrimination* (pp. 89–99). New York, NY: Psychology Press.

Ngo, J., & Nip, A. (2011, April 30). Visitors wander streets at night after row with tour guide. *South China Morning Post*, City 1.

Pearce, P. L. (1982). *The social psychology of tourist behaviour* (Vol. 3). New York, NY: Pergamon Press.

Philipp, S. F. (1994). Race and tourism choice: A legacy of discrimination? *Annals of Tourism Research, 21*(3), 479–488.

Phinney, J. S., Madden, T., & Santos, L. J. (1998). Psychological variables as predictors of perceived ethnic discrimination among minority and immigrant adolescents. *Journal of Applied Social Psychology, 28*(11), 937–953.

Redmond, M. V. (2000). Cultural distance as a mediating factor between stress and intercultural communication competence. *International Journal of Intercultural Relations, 24*(1), 151–159.

Reisinger, Y., & Turner, L. W. (2002). Cultural differences between Asian tourist markets and Australian hosts: Part 2. *Journal of Travel Research, 40*(4), 385–395.

Reisinger, Y., & Turner, L. W. (2003). *Cross-cultural behaviour in tourism: Concepts and analysis.* Oxford, England: Butterworth-Heinemann.

Sandhu, D. S., & Asrabadi, B. R. (1994). Development of an acculturative stress scale for international students: Preliminary findings. *Psychological Reports, 75*, 435–449.

Sellers, R. M., & Shelton, J. N. (2003). The role of racial identity in perceived racial discrimination. *Journal of Personality and Social Psychology, 84*(5), 1079–1092.

Sharma, P., Tam, J. L. M., & Kim, N. (2009). Demystifying intercultural service encounters: Toward a comprehensive conceptual framework. *Journal of Service Research, 12*(2), 227–242.

Sherif, M., & Hovland, C. I. (1961). *Social judgment: Assimilation and contrast effects in communication and attitude change.* New Haven, CT: Yale University Press.

Smart, J., & Smart, D. W. (1995). Acculturative stress of hispanics: Loss and challenge. *Journal of Counseling and Development, 73*(4), 390–396.

Spencer-Rodgers, J., & McGovern, T. (2002). Attitudes toward the culturally different: The role of intercultural communication barriers, affective responses, consensual stereotypes, and perceived threat. *International Journal of Intercultural Relations, 26*(6), 609–631.

Taylor, S. E., Peplau, L. A., & Sears, D. O. (2006). *Social psychology* (Vol. 12). Upper Saddle River, NJ: Pearson Prentice Hall.

Thornicroft, G., Brohan, E., Rose, D., Sartorius, N., & Leese, M. (2009). Global pattern of experienced and anticipated discrimination against people with schizophrenia: A cross-sectional survey. *The Lancet, 373*(9661), 408–415.

Walsh, G. (2009). Disadvantaged consumers' experiences of marketplace discrimination in customer services. *Journal of Marketing Management, 25*(1), 143–169.

Wan, K. (2012, March 2). Mainlanders are part of same family. *South China Morning Post*, EDT 18.

Ward, C., & Kennedy, A. (1999). The measurement of sociocultural adaptation. *International Journal of Intercultural Relations, 23*(4), 659–677.

Wei, L., Crompton, J. L., & Reid, L. M. (1989). Cultural conflicts: Experiences of U.S. visitors to China. *Tourism Management, 10*(4), 322–332.

Willming, C. L. (2001). *Leisure-travel behaviors of college-educated African Americans and perceived racial discrimination* (Doctoral dissertation, University of Florida). Retrieved from ProQuest Dissertations & Theses Database. (Accession Order No. AAT 3027619)

Ye, H., Zhang, H. Q., & Yuen, P. P. (in press). Perceived discrimination in the context of high and low interactions—Evidence from medical and general tourists. *Asia Pacific Journal of Tourism Research.*

Zeithaml, V. A., Berry, L., & Parasuraman, A. (1993). The nature and determinants of customer expectations of service. *Journal of the Academy of Marketing Science, 21*(1), 1–12.

Zhang, H. Q., & Lam, T. (1999). An analysis of Mainland Chinese visitors' motivations to visit Hong Kong. *Tourism Management, 20*(5), 587–594.

From Destination Image to Destination Loyalty: Evidence From Recreation Farms in Taiwan

从目的地意象到目的地忠诚之模式探讨：以台湾休闲农场为例

CHYONG-RU LIU
WEI-RONG LIN
YAO-CHIN WANG

With the rising popularity of recreation farms in Taiwan, understanding visitors' behavior is a critical issue. Therefore, this study attempts to establish a model that includes destination image, self-congruity, destination personality, and destination loyalty to clarify the mechanism from image to loyalty. Yilan Shangrila Recreation Farm was selected as the research setting and 326 usable responses were received. The results revealed that destination image shows positive impacts on self-congruity, destination personality, and destination loyalty. However, there was no significant relationship between self-congruity and destination loyalty. Further analysis showed the existence of significant differences between first-time and repeat visitors. The path from destination image to destination personality to destination loyalty can better explain how image leads to loyalty. The findings of this study provide meaningful academic and managerial implications.

休闲农场在台湾正逐渐受到民众喜爱，而了解游客行为模式将成为重要议题。因此，本研究将建立一个包含目的地意象、自我一致性、目的地个性以及目的地忠诚的模式以厘清意象到忠诚之间的脉络机制。本研究以台湾宜兰香格里拉休闲农场为调查场域，针对现场游客进行问卷调查，共收回三百二十六份有效问卷。研究结果显示目的地意象会正向影响自我一致性、目的地个性以及目的地忠诚。然而，自我一致性与目的地忠诚之间并不存在显著关系，惟进一步分析指出，初游者与重游者却有不一样的结果。本研究模式有助于了解意象是如何影响到忠诚，最后提出学术与管理意涵。

关键词： 目的地意象，目的地个性，自我一致性，目的地忠诚，台湾休闲农场

Chyong-Ru Liu is Associate Professor in the Graduate Institute of Environment, Recreation and Tourism at National Changhua University of Education, Changhua City, Taiwan.

Wei-Rong Lin is a PhD candidate at the Graduate Institute of Recreation, Tourism and Hospitality Management at National Chiayi University, Chiayi City, Taiwan.

Yao-Chin Wang is a PhD student in the School of Hotel and Restaurant Administration at Oklahoma State University, Stillwater, OK, USA.

Introduction

In 2010, the Taiwanese Recreation Farming Development Association reported that Taiwan has 239 legal recreation farms where visitors can enjoy the relaxing countryside lifestyle, participate in traditional culture and agricultural arts, or experience the beautiful natural resources of Taiwan. Recreation farms elicit images of birds, clean streams, unpolluted crops, a healthy atmosphere, and fresh air. Most recreation farms in the Taiwanese farming industry share a similar image and lack unique features with which tourists can identify. Thus, retaining customer loyalty is an important task for farm managers.

Destination image is defined as tourists' impressions of a particular destination (Crompton, 1979). Leisen (2001) noted that destination image can help visitors to select a destination from among many possible choices. Destination image represents the image of a destination in the mind of the tourist (Fakeye & Crompton, 1991) and is positively related to revisit intention (Chen & Tsai, 2007; Chi & Qu, 2008). *Destination personality* has also been defined as a set of human characteristics associated with a destination (Ekinci & Hosany, 2006). Ekinci, Sirakaya-Turk, and Baloglu (2007) and Usakli and Baloglu (2011) agreed that destination personality efficiently improves the revisit intentions of tourists and word-of-mouth reputation. Thus, farm managers in Taiwan should strive to establish a unique destination image and unique personality to attract repeat visits by tourists.

Exploring the mechanism by which destination image translates into destination loyalty requires a discussion of destination personality and self-congruity. *Self-congruity* is the congruence between a destination image and a visitor's self-image (Sirgy & Su, 2000). Sirgy and Su (2000) adopted an integrative model to discuss relationships among destination image, self-congruity, and travel behavior. Kressmann et al. (2006) demonstrated the direct and indirect effect of self-image congruence on brand loyalty. Many studies have also attempted to explain how travel behavior is affected by destination image (Chen & Tsai, 2007; Lin, Morais, Kerstetter, & Hou, 2007; Tasci & Gartner, 2007), destination personality (Ekinci & Hosany, 2006; Usakli & Baloglu, 2011), or self-congruity (Beerli, Meneses, & Gil, 2007; Kastenholz, 2004; Litvin & Goh, 2002). However, few studies have discussed the relationships between destination image, destination personality, self-congruity, and destination loyalty in the field of recreation farms. Furthermore, through a review of 142 papers on destination image analysis published during 1973 to 2000, Pike (2002) found that most studies in this field focus first on countries as destinations (e.g., Hosany, Ekinci, & Uysal, 2006), followed by states (e.g., Murphy, Benckendorff, & Moscardo, 2007) or cities (e.g., Usakli & Baloglu, 2011). Recreation farms are rarely reported on in the literature. Whether the results of previous studies are applicable to recreation farms has not been studied.

The purpose of this study is to discuss the relationships between destination image, destination personality, self-congruity, and destination loyalty based on visitor perceptions of recreations farms. Research models based on these four constructs are rarely reported. Some studies have examined the relationship between two constructs such as that between destination image and destination loyalty (Beerli & Martín, 2004; Bigne, Sanchez, & Sanchez, 2001) or the relationship between destination personality and self-congruity (Usakli & Baloglu, 2011). Specifically, the research model used both destination personality and self-congruity to clarify the effects of destination image on destination loyalty. The research questionnaire items were revised by managers of the recreation farms. We also cooperated with one of the most famous recreation farms in Taiwan, the

Yilan Shangrila Recreation Farm, and conducted field research there. Meaningful data were obtained to help answer the research questions. Destination loyalty is closely related to sustainable profitability and is a central goal for most of the recreation farms focused on the revisit market. Responses from on-site visitors provide direct information about the foundations of their loyalty and what managers should do to improve that loyalty.

Finally, the focus on recreation farming in Taiwan offers several advantages. First, reports from the Taiwan Council of Agriculture (2010) mentioned that visitors to recreation farms in Taiwan number over 10 million. Raising the standards of the agricultural industry and increasing added value are admittedly not prioritized in Taiwan. Recreation farming should be a key focus of these efforts. Second, the trend of recreation farming has spread from the West to Asia and from Taiwan to China. Empirical studies of recreation farming in Taiwan can also provide useful lessons for other countries in attempts to develop recreation farming.

Literature Review and Hypothesis

The Role of Destination Image

Crompton (1979) defined *destination image* as a tourist's beliefs, knowledge, and impressions of a particular destination. Moreover, Sirgy and Su (2000) pointed out that destination image is tourists' positive evaluation of a destination. A high destination image indicates that tourists perceive the positive attributes of the destination.

Destination images result from three distinctly different but hierarchically interrelated components: cognitive, affective, and conative components (Gartner, 1993). The cognitive image component is defined as an intellectual evaluation of the known attributes or understanding of the product. The affective image component is related to the underlying motives for selecting the destination. The conative image component is analogous to behavior because it is the action component. However, Hosany et al. (2006) suggested that destination personality has a stronger relationship with the affective component of destination image. Additionally, destination loyalty results from personal behavior that reflects the conative component of destination image. Thus, this study avoids overlap between destination image and other constructs that influence clarification of the research model by applying cognitive image as the operational definition of destination image, which is the typical approach observed in the literature (Castro, Armario, & Ruiz, 2007; Leisen, 2001).

According to Kressmann et al. (2006), *self-congruity* is the match between the consumer's self-concept and the user's image of a given product or brand. According to Sirgy (1985), self-concept consists of four major concepts: actual self-image, ideal self-image, social self-image, and ideal social self-image. An *actual self-image* is an actual self-perception. An *ideal self-image* is how a person would like to perceive himself or herself. A *social self-image* is how an individual thinks he or she is perceived by others, and an *ideal social self-image* is how the individual desires to be perceived by others.

Sirgy (1985) added that congruence between self-image and product image improves customer attitudes and behaviors related to a product because it influences their product preference and purchase intentions. Sirgy and Su (2000) developed a destination image model that integrated the relationships among destination environment, destination visitor image, tourist self-concept, self-congruity, functional congruity, and travel behavior. A review of the tourism literature by Beerli et al. (2007) revealed a tendency to characterize destinations as human-like and to explain tourist visit intentions as a process of congruity between their self-concept and perceived destination image. Additionally, Hung and Petrick (2011) found that the congruency between tourists' self-images and their images of a destination increases their probability of visiting. Based on the reasoning presented in this study, we hypothesize the following:

H1: Destination image positively impacts self-congruity.

Tasci and Gartner (2007) noted that some destination image studies treat destination image as an independent variable influencing several customer behavior variables, such as intention to visit (Leisen, 2001), recommend (Ross, 1993), or revisit (Rittichainuwat, Qu, & Brown, 2001). Tourists who perceive a destination positively are more likely to visit that destination (Birgit, 2001). Additionally, destination image can positively influence tourists' experiences, satisfaction, and behavioral intentions (Bigne et al., 2001). Chen and Tsai (2007) also found that destination image significantly and positively affects behavioral intention. Lin et al. (2007) demonstrated that overall destination image is an important antecedent of tourist destination preferences; moreover, the importance of cognitive image and affective image varies among different destinations. Dick and Basu (1994) explained that cognitive, affective, and conative antecedents can stimulate customers' relative attitudes, and those relative attitudes then enhance customer repeat patronage or increase the consequences of the loyalty relationship in the same way as word-of-mouth advertising. Promoting destination image can enhance customer perceptions of the antecedents of relative attitudes toward the destination, thus resulting in customer repeat patronage. Furthermore, Govers, Go, and Kumar (2007) found that successful marketing communication strategies can significantly influence travel behavior, further demonstrating the influence of destination image on destination loyalty. Therefore, this study hypothesizes the following:

H2: Destination image positively impacts destination loyalty.

Brand personality is defined as "the set of human characteristics associated with a brand" (Aaker, 1997, p. 347). Aaker (1997) developed five dimensions of brand personality: sincerity, excitement, competence, sophistication, and ruggedness. Geuens, Weijters, and Wulf (2009) measured brand personality using another five dimensions: responsibility, activity, aggressiveness, simplicity, and emotionality. To assess consumer perceptions of brand personality appeal, Freling, Crosno, and Henard (2011) validated measures of brand personality appeal using the three dimensions of favorability, originality, and clarity. Furthermore, Freling and Forbes (2005) found that brand personality is connected to numerous other brand associations in consumer memory and is accessible through spreading activation. The natural human tendency is for consumers to embrace brands with strong, positive personalities (Freling & Forbes, 2005). Thus, managers should know how to manage the consistency and coherence of brand image across different market segments and over long periods (Van Rekom, Jacobs, & Verlegh, 2006). The obvious importance of brand personalities has led many researchers to continue research in this field to develop new measures (Freling & Forbes, 2005; Geuens et al., 2009; Van Rekom et al., 2006).

In fact, the concept of destination personality is the same as that of brand personality, because tourism destinations can be considered as brands. Applying the definition of Aaker (1997), Hosany et al. (2006) defined *destination personality* as "the set of human characteristics associated with a tourism destination" (p. 639) and found that destination image and destination personality are related concepts because the emotional component of destination image captures most variance in destination personality. Moreover, Ekinci et al. (2007) demonstrated that destination image positively influences destination personality. Regarding the gaming destination image perspective, Kneesel, Baloglu, and Millar (2010) found that well-known destination brands are associated with high awareness and familiarity, more positive overall image, and more affective descriptions. Thus, destination personality is realized more clearly if more people can perceive the destination image. Accordingly, we hypothesize the following:

H3: Destination image positively impacts destination personality.

Relationships Among Destination Personality, Self-Congruity, and Destination Loyalty

Usakli and Baloglu (2011) showed that self-congruity has a partial mediating effect between destination personality and behavioral intentions; that is, through self-congruity, destination personality indirectly but positively affects the intention to return to and recommend a destination. Similarly, Ekinci (2003) proposed that brand personality is significantly related to self-image congruence. Moreover, Murphy et al. (2007) indicated that the congruity between tourists' self-image and their perceptions of a destination is high when they associate the destination with a destination brand personality and when the association is consistent with their desired travel experience. Customers who easily perceive a destination personality easily identify aspects of the destination that match with their actual or ideal self-image (Baloglu & McCleary, 1999; Bao, Bao, & Sheng, 2011; Litvin & Goh, 2002; Sirgy, 1985). Thus, how to manipulate the impression of a brand personality and how to help customers match a destination personality with self-image in self-congruity is an important research issue (Johar, Sengupta, & Aaker, 2005). Based on the reasoning outlined here, we hypothesize the following:

H4: Destination personality positively impacts self-congruity.

Goh and Litvin (2000) and Litvin and Goh (2002) found that self-congruity effectively predicts destination choice. Additionally, Helgeson and Supphellen (2004) demonstrated that self-congruity independently affects brand attitude. Sirgy and Su (2000) also mentioned that self-congruity denotes the match between destination image and a tourist's self-concept, where a closer match increases tourists' likelihood of visiting. Furthermore, Beerli et al. (2007) suggested that tourists' power to predict destination choice increases with their involvement in leisure tourism. In addition, Beerli et al. (2007) found that self-congruity loses its determining power after tourists have already visited a place. Nevertheless, the findings of Beerli et al. (2007) differed from those of Sirgy, Lee, Johar, and Tidwell (2008); the latter found that self-congruity with a sponsorship event positively influences brand loyalty. Additionally, Kressmann et al. (2006) noted the paramount importance of self-congruity in predicting brand loyalty. To further understand the relationship between self-congruity and loyalty intention, this study hypothesizes the following:

H5: Self-congruity positively impacts destination loyalty.

Ekinci et al. (2007) noted that destination image positively influences destination personality and thus influences tourist loyalty through destination personality. Sung and

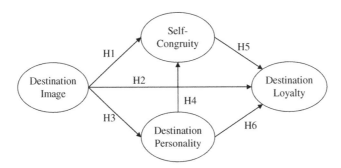

Figure 1. Conceptual model.

Kim (2010) found that the sincerity and ruggedness dimensions of brand personality are more likely to influence brand trust, whereas the excitement and sophistication dimensions are more closely related to brand affect. The findings demonstrated that brand personality increases brand trust and evokes brand affect, in turn increasing brand loyalty (Sung & Kim, 2010). Furthermore, Helgeson and Supphellen (2004) demonstrated that destination personality independently affects brand attitude. Additionally, Swaminathan, Stilley, and Ahluwalia (2009) mentioned that customers are likely to have higher loyalty intentions when they are under high avoidance and high anxiety. In fact, perceptions of destination personality can reduce information asymmetry, increasing tourist knowledge of destinations and helping them evaluate their destination identification (Ekinci & Hosany, 2006; Freling et al., 2011). According to the framework of customer loyalty proposed by Dick and Basu (1994), destination personality can be seen as an affective antecedent that enhances customers' attitudes toward a destination and thus increases repeat patronage. For this reason, Govers et al. (2007) stressed the importance of consistency and coherence in marketing communications regarding a destination, because these can maintain the identification of existing customers and thus their loyalty intention. Given the above, we hypothesize the following:

H6: Destination personality positively impacts destination loyalty.

This study examines the relationships among destination image, self-congruity, destination personality, and destination loyalty in tourists visiting recreation farms. Figure 1 shows the comprehensive theoretical model established in this study.

Method

Sample and Data Collection

The target population of this study comprised visitors to recreation farms in Taiwan, and Yilan Shangrila Recreation Farm was selected as the research setting. A convenience sampling method, by which the most conveniently available units (or people) were sampled (Zikmund, 2003), was used. Self-administered questionnaires were distributed to visitors at the farm exit. Data collection was conducted over 12 weeks from February to April 2010. Sampling was performed two times each week, once on a weekday and once on the weekend. Some 326 usable responses were ultimately obtained from a total of 350 self-administered questionnaires.

The sample included slightly more female respondents (58.9%) than males. Respondent ages ranged from 18 to 65 years old, with a mean of 39.9 years old. Most of the respondents (55.5%) were from northern Taiwan, and approximately 63.8% held a bachelor's degree. In terms of income, most respondents (35.9%) had incomes between US$600–1,300 per month. About half of the respondents (50.9%) were visiting Yilan Shangrila Recreation Farm for the first time in the past 3 years. Over half of the respondents (58.3%) traveled with friends, and 35.0% traveled with family. Finally, 44.8% of the respondents were on trips lasting one day, and 42.9% were on trips lasting 2 days.

Measurement

The study constructs (destination image, destination personality, self-congruity, and behavioral intentions) were operationalized using items from previous empirical studies. The following information describes the scale items used for construct measurement in the study model.

Measurement items modified from Beerli and Martín (2004) were used to measure destination image. A farm manager and the secretary director of the Taiwan Leisure Farms Development Association were also invited to modify items to improve the model fit to data collected for the Taiwanese Leisure Farm. Most items in destination image relate to cognitive image. Four dimensions underlining destination image were natural and cultural resources (three items), atmosphere (three items), social setting and environment (three items), and leisure infrastructure (three items). These items were rated using a 5-point Likert scale ranging from 1 (*strongly disagree*) to 5 (*strongly agree*).

Destination personality was captured using personality traits derived from the unique personality trait generation stage. The destination personality scale proposed by Usakli and Baloglu (2011) was used to measure the destination personality of the recreation farm in this study. The five dimensions used were sincerity, excitement, competence, sophistication, and ruggedness. Fifteen destination personality items were measured on a 5-point Likert scale ranging from 1 (*strongly disagree*) to 5 (*strongly agree*).

Self-congruity was derived from previous research by Sirgy et al. (1997), Sirgy and Su (2000), and Helgeson and Supphellen (2004). These congruity statements were measured using a 5-point Likert scale ranging from 1 (*strongly disagree*) to 5 (*strongly agree*).

Regarding destination loyalty, attitudinal measurements, including repeat purchase intentions and recommendations, were usually used to infer consumer loyalty. Therefore, repurchase and referral intentions comprise the bulk of customer loyalty intention (Taylor, 1998). This study adapted the scale from Chi and Qu (2008) and used two single-item measures to assess tourist destination loyalty as the ultimate dependent construct—tourist intention to revisit a recreation farm and their willingness to recommend a recreation farm—using a 5-point Likert scale ranging from 1 (*strongly disagree*) to 5 (*strongly agree*).

The survey instrument was originally prepared in English and then back-translated into Mandarin (Parameswaran & Yaprak, 1987). The survey instrument was tested using a pilot sample of 60 visitors. Visitors had no difficulty understanding the survey items and thus there was no compelling reason to change the survey instrument.

Additionally, the questionnaire items were revised by several top managers of recreation farms to ensure that the measurement reflected reality.

Results

Following Anderson and Gerbing (1988), this study adopted a two-stage confirmatory factor analysis to test whether all of the dimensions demonstrated sufficient convergent and discriminant validity (Table 1). The results indicated acceptable psychometric properties (Bentler & Wu, 1993). For example, χ^2/df ($df = 440$) = 2.22, goodness of fit index (GFI) = 0.85, standardized root mean square residual (SRMR) = 0.041, root mean square of error approximation (RMSEA) = 0.061, nonnormed fit index (NNFI) = 0.98, and comparative fit index (CFI) = 0.98, and the t values for the factor loadings of all the measurement items reached significance ($p < .05$). These results indicated acceptable combination reliability (CR), average variance extracted (AVE), and convergent validity for all dimensions.

Discriminant validity is indicated if the square roots of the AVE of the dimensions exceed the correlations of other dimensions (Fornell & Larcker, 1981). Table 2 shows that all square roots of the AVE of the dimensions exceeded 0.75 in this study. The strongest correlation between the dimensions was 0.74, which supported discriminant validity.

Reliability and validity were acceptable for all of the study dimensions, implying that it is viable to use a single measurement indicator rather than multiple such indicators (Homburg, Grozdanovic, & Klarmann, 2007). The average of the dimension scores of the destination image and destination personality measurement patterns during the first stage were taken and adopted as the multiple measurement indicator during the second stage.

Structural modeling can be performed using preliminary fit criteria, overall model fit, and internal model fit (Bagozzi & Yi, 1988). Notably, the analytical results suggested that this investigation identified three basic fitness indicators (Wu & Liang, 2011):

1. No significant negative value.
2. Factor loading not below 0.5 or above 0.95.
3. Tests of the hypotheses reach significance.

All three standards were met and generally accepted, as shown in Table 3. The overall fit measures indicated that the hypothesized model accurately represented the structure underlying the observed data, χ^2/df ($df = 84$) = 2.04, GFI = 0.93, SRMR = 0.034, RMSEA = 0.057, NNFI = 0.99, and CFI = 0.99. Internal structural fit was assessed using the following criteria: (a) individual reliability exceeding 0.5, (b) reliability of potential variable combination exceeding 0.7, and (c) AVE of potential variance exceeding 0.5. Table 3 shows that the AVE fell between 0.54 and 0.77. Overall, the analytical results suggested that all indicators were acceptable, revealing good internal structural fitness.

Figure 2 and Table 4 show that destination image significantly and positively influenced self-congruity ($\gamma = 0.42$), destination personality ($\gamma = 0.32$), and destination loyalty ($\gamma = 0.81$), supporting hypotheses 1, 2, and 3. Additionally, destination personality positively influenced self-congruity ($\beta = 0.39$) and destination loyalty ($\beta = 0.34$), supporting hypotheses 4 and 6. However, self-congruity did not positively influence destination loyalty ($\beta = 0.09$) and, thus, hypothesis 5 is not supported. Furthermore, the

Table 1. Results of Measurement Model Analysis.

Dimensions	Items	Mean	Standardized Loadings	CR	Average
Natural and cultural resources (DI1)				0.83	0.61
	Diversity of the natural resources	4.07	0.76		
	Appeal of the scenery	4.25	0.77		
	Attraction of the farming culture	4.11	0.82		
Atmosphere (DI2)				0.84	0.64
	Fresh air	4.39	0.79		
	Opportunity for leisure experience	4.21	0.80		
	Clean tourism environment	4.17	0.81		
Leisure infrastructures (DI3)				0.81	0.59
	Sound tourism facilities	4.00	0.78		
	Provide beverage and food	3.95	0.78		
	Provide local souvenirs	3.59	0.74		
Social setting and environment (DI4)				0.81	0.59
	Place for family tourism	4.17	0.79		
	Place for outdoor teaching	4.06	0.81		
	Place for idle play	3.77	0.71		
Sincerity (DP1)				0.84	0.57
	Honest	4.22	0.78		
	Down-to-earth	4.29	0.78		
	Wholesome	4.47	0.70		
	Cheerful	4.33	0.76		
Excitement (DP2)				0.86	0.60
	Up-to-date	3.50	0.77		
	Spirited	4.04	0.77		
	Daring	3.93	0.77		
	Imaginative	3.88	0.78		

(Continued)

Table 1. Continued.

Dimensions	Items	Mean	Standardized Loadings	CR	Average
Competence (DP3)				0.79	0.56
	Reliable	4.07	0.73		
	Intelligent	4.04	0.73		
	Successful	3.86	0.79		
Sophistication (DP4)				0.82	0.70
	Upper class	4.07	0.81		
	Charming	3.95	0.86		
Ruggedness (DP5)				0.76	0.61
	Outdoorsy	4.47	0.75		
	Tough	4.20	0.81		
Self-congruity (SC)				0.93	0.78
	Recreation farm is consistent with how I see myself	3.90	0.86		
	I am quite similar to the image of the recreation farm	3.82	0.84		
	Recreation farm is consistent with how I would like to see myself	3.81	0.91		
	I would like to be perceived as similar to the image of the recreation farm	3.73	0.91		
Destination loyalty (DL)				0.88	0.78
	I will revisit the recreation farm	3.97	0.88		
	I will recommend the recreation farm as a favorable destination to others	4.03	0.89		

Table 2. Results of Discriminant Validity Tests.

	DI1	DI2	DI3	DI4	DP1	DP2	DP3	DP4	DP5	SC	DL
DI1	0.78										
DI2	0.70	0.80									
DI3	0.71	0.64	0.77								
DI4	0.66	0.62	0.74	0.77							
DP1	0.56	0.47	0.51	0.48	0.75						
DP2	0.53	0.39	0.56	0.52	0.53	0.77					
DP3	0.52	0.42	0.54	0.48	0.61	0.68	0.75				
DP4	0.50	0.45	0.49	0.46	0.56	0.50	0.52	0.84			
DP5	0.54	0.45	0.48	0.52	0.51	0.48	0.48	0.52	0.78		
SC	0.57	0.48	0.66	0.60	0.52	0.55	0.58	0.49	0.48	0.88	
DL	0.51	0.49	0.45	0.48	0.47	0.44	0.46	0.45	0.41	0.49	0.88

Note. The diagonal elements are the square root of the average variance extracted. The off-diagonal elements are the correlations between the constructs ($p < .05$).

Table 3. Results of Structural Model Analysis.

Dimensions	Items	Standardized Loadings	CR	Average
Destination image			0.89	0.67
	DI1	0.83		
	DI2	0.76		
	DI3	0.86		
	DI4	0.82		
Destination personality			0.86	0.54
	DP1	0.76		
	DP2	0.76		
	DP3	0.79		
	DP4	0.70		
	DP5	0.67		
Self-congruity			0.93	0.78
	SC1	0.86		
	SC2	0.84		
	SC3	0.91		
	SC4	0.91		
Destination loyalty			0.87	0.77
	DL1	0.89		
	DL2	0.87		

variances of self-congruity, destination personality, and destination loyalty were 60, 66, and 50%, respectively.

Table 5 shows three indirect paths between destination image and destination loyalty with destination personality and self-congruity as mediators. First, the direct influence of destination image on self-congruity was 0.42 (standard error [SE] = 0.09),

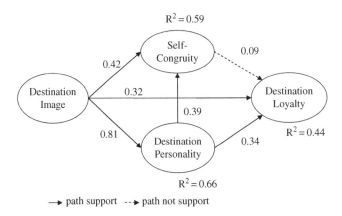

Figure 2. Path analysis of the structural equation model.

Table 4. Path Analysis of Research Framework.

Hypothesis	Path	Standard $\beta(t)$	Support or Not
H1	Destination image → Self-congruity	0.42 (4.57)	Support
H2	Destination image → Destination loyalty	0.32 (2.96)	Support
H3	Destination image → Destination personality	0.81 (12.52)	Support
H4	Destination personality → Self-congruity	0.39 (4.21)	Support
H5	Self-congruity → Destination loyalty	0.09 (1.15)	Not
H6	Destination personality → Destination loyalty	0.34 (3.03)	Support

Table 5. Path Analysis of Indirect Effects.

Path	Standard β	Sobel's Test
DI → SC → DL	0.038	1.09
DI → DP →DL	0.275	2.98
DI → DP → SC → DL	0.028	0.74

and the direct influence of self-congruity on destination loyalty was 0.09 ($SE = 0.08$). The indirect effect of the relationship was 0.038, and the Z value was 1.09 ($p > .05$) according to the Sobel test (Sobel, 1982). Thus, destination image may not influence destination loyalty through self-congruity. Second, the direct relationship between destination image and destination personality was 0.81 ($SE = 0.07$), and the direct relationship between destination personality and destination loyalty was 0.34 ($SE =$

Table 6. Results of Hypothesis 5 for First-Time and Repeat Visitors.

	N	Self-Congruity → Destination Loyalty Standard β(t)	Support or Not	Model Fit
First-time visitors	162	0.19 (2.21)	Support	χ^2/df $(df = 84) = 1.55$, GFI $= 0.90$, RMSEA $= 0.059$, CFI $= 0.99$
Repeat visitors	160	−0.09 (−0.02)	Not	χ^2/df $(df = 84) = 1.45$, GFI $= 0.91$, RMSEA $= 0.053$, CFI $= 0.99$

0.11). The indirect effect of the relationship was 0.275 and the Z value was 2.98 ($p < .05$) according to the Sobel test (Sobel, 1982). Thus, the data confirmed that destination image affects destination loyalty through destination personality. Third, the direct influence of destination image on destination personality was 0.81 ($SE = 0.07$), the direct influence of destination personality on self-congruity was 0.39 ($SE = 0.09$), and the direct influence of self-congruity on destination loyalty was 0.09 ($SE = 0.08$). The indirect effect of the relationship above was 0.028 and the Z value was 0.74 ($p > .05$) according to the Sobel test (Sobel, 1982). Thus, destination image may not influence destination loyalty through both destination personality and self-congruity.

Furthermore, this investigation separated the data into first-time and repeat visitors based on visit experience to understand why hypothesis 5 is insignificant. The sample size of the two groups was 162 and 160, respectively. A structural equation modeling analysis was performed to test hypothesis 5 separately for these two groups (see Table 6). For first-time visitors, self-congruity was positively related to destination loyalty ($\beta = 0.19$, $p < .05$), indicating that the structural model had adequate fit. In contrast, based on the structural model having an adequate fit, no significant relationship existed between self-congruity and destination loyalty ($\beta = -0.09$, $p > .05$) for repeat visitors. The results indicated that visit experience moderates the relationship between self-congruity and destination loyalty.

Discussion and Conclusion

This study discussed the relationships between destination image, self-congruity, destination personality, and destination loyalty. The results revealed that destination image is positively related to self-congruity, destination personality, and destination loyalty. Furthermore, destination personality is positively related to self-congruity and destination loyalty. These findings indicate that destination image can enhance tourist perceptions of destination personality, thus increasing their loyalty intentions. Surprisingly, the empirical results revealed no relationship between self-congruity and destination loyalty. Thus, in explaining the mechanism from image to loyalty, destination personality is a better mediator than self-congruity and demonstrates how image leads to tourist destination loyalty.

The positive influence of destination image on self-congruity is consistent with the previous findings of Sirgy and Su (2000), Litvin and Goh (2002), Kastenholz (2004), and Bao et al. (2011). Tourists can match dimensions like natural and cultural resources, atmosphere, social setting and environment, and leisure infrastructure with their ideal and actual selves. Furthermore, destination image positively influences destination loyalty. Cognition of a positive image can stimulate tourist motivation and increase tourists' desire to visit a destination (Bigne et al., 2001; Lin et al., 2007; Tasci, 2009; Tasci & Gartner, 2007). As mentioned by Chen and Tsai (2007), destination image can influence behavioral intention directly, not just indirectly. Additionally, destination image is strongly and positively related to destination personality. This study measured destination image using cognitive images. Destination cognition influences emotional components like tourists' perceptions of a destination's personality (Ekinci et al., 2007; Hosany et al., 2006; Kneesel et al., 2010).

This study also found a positive relationship between destination personality and self-congruity. This finding implies that destination image influences self-congruity not only directly but also indirectly through destination personality (Ekinci, 2003). Furthermore, destination personality is significantly related to destination loyalty. This relationship perfectly explains the indirect impact of destination image on destination loyalty. Numerous studies also mentioned that destination or brand personality influences customers' behavioral intentions (Ekinci & Hosany, 2006; Ekinci et al., 2007; Freling et al., 2011; Helgeson & Supphellen, 2004; Sung & Kim, 2010).

Nevertheless, the findings of the study indicate that self-congruity is not related to destination loyalty. This result contradicts previous studies on both product markets (Helgeson & Supphellen, 2004; Kressmann et al., 2006) and tourism markets (Goh & Litvin, 2000; Litvin & Goh, 2002; Sirgy & Su, 2000). Numerous possible explanations exist for this unexpected finding. First, Beerli et al. (2007) found that self-congruity may lose its determining power in the case of repeat visitors. This study found that just 50.9% of respondents were first-time visitors to the Yilan Shangrila Recreation Farm. Tourists who have visited a recreation farm more than twice have already established relevant cognition. Thus, affective factors or emotional components (e.g., destination personality) may be more effective in maintaining existing tourists (Hosany et al., 2006). To further examine the explanation of tourism experience presented in this study, the differences between first-time and repeat visitors were tested in terms of the relationship between self-congruity and destination loyalty (see Table 5). The results revealed significant differences between first-time and repeat visitors in terms of the effect of self-congruity on destination loyalty. For first-time visitors, self-congruity was positively related to destination loyalty, but no significant relationship existed between self-congruity and destination loyalty for repeat visitors. Second, Lin et al. (2007) demonstrated that the importance of cognitive and affective image varies across different destinations (natural, developed, and theme park destinations). This phenomenon demonstrates that for recreation farming, cognitive images influence destination loyalty more through destination personality than self-congruity. That is, in recreation farming, cognitive factors should arouse affective factors and thus improve loyalty. Such an explanation may stress the importance of the changing effects of cognitive and affective factors in different destinations, as noted by Lin et al. (2007).

Academic Implications

Initially, the path from destination image and destination personality to destination loyalty is the main means by which the proposed model explains how destination image influences destination loyalty. Winning tourist loyalty requires improved destination image so that cognitive factors positively influence affective or emotional factors, which in turn stimulate tourists' behavioral intentions. The findings of this study show that self-congruity does not result in a significant association between image and loyalty because it seldom arouses affective or emotional factors in tourists. High self-congruity with a destination image may motivate a first-time visit to a destination (Goh & Litvin, 2000; Litvin & Goh, 2002; Sirgy & Su, 2000). For tourists who have already visited the destination, however, associated cognition is already established. Thus, affective or emotional variables such as destination personality should be emphasized to motivate tourists' behavioral intentions (Hosany et al., 2006).

On the other hand, the nonsignificant effect of self-congruity on destination loyalty in this study reflects the need to explore the changing role of cognitive and affective factors in predicting destination loyalty across different destinations (Lin et al., 2007). In the case of recreation farms, cognitive images like traditional cultural or natural resources come to mind more easily than affective images. Nevertheless, visitors considering island tourism may perceive more affective images related to such destinations. Cognitive and affective factors seem to play different roles in different destinations, because different destinations are associated with different compositions of cognitive and affective images.

Managerial Implications

Managers of recreation farms should pursue differentiation to achieve destination loyalty. Without differentiation, it is hard for tourists to identify specific destinations from among numerous others with similar offerings. Thus, recreation farms must establish a destination personality to shape their own specializations and touch the hearts of tourists (Hoeffler & Keller, 2003; Morgan & Pritchard, 2002). Managers of recreation farms should become storytellers and tell stories about their farms based on their destination image and personality. They must combine existing resources with local resources, culture, and history to create a positive and distinctive image and personality for the recreation farms. Doing so helps to maintain tourist loyalty because the self-congruity of some tourists matches the unique image or personality of the destination.

Furthermore, Govers et al. (2007) stressed the importance of consistency and coherence in marketing communications for keeping the attention of existing customers and maintaining their destination loyalty. Managers of recreation farms should enhance their destination personality in marketing to improve tourist identification with the destination. Furthermore, Kneesel et al. (2010) added that well-known destination brands are associated with high awareness and familiarity, more positive images, and more affective descriptions, thus achieving a halo effect in terms of the evaluation of cognitive attributes, visit intention, and word of mouth.

Managers should develop different strategies depending on whether their target market is first-time or repeat visitors. As mentioned by Morais and Lin (2010), an effective means of enhancing patronage of a destination involves more information processing for first-time visitors and enhanced customer relationships with repeat visitors. Information processing can provide more cognitive images for first-time visitors and promote the path from destination image to self-congruity to destination loyalty. Furthermore, customer relationship management can enhance customers' affective linkage with the destination and strengthen destination personality, thus increasing destination loyalty among repeat visitors.

Future Research

This study developed a model that includes destination image, destination personality, self-congruity, and destination loyalty. By focusing on recreation farms, this article found that destination personality is an important variable in explaining the influence of destination image on destination loyalty. As mentioned at the beginning of this study, recreation farms in Taiwan have similar images, making segmentation necessary to win tourist loyalty. Thus, destination personality is more efficient than self-congruity in maintaining tourist revisit intention and can arouse more affective factors associated with the destination (Freling & Forbes, 2005; Kneesel et al., 2010). The nonsignificant relationship between self-congruity and loyalty may also have resulted from the measurement of cognitive destination image. Measurements of multiple images are needed in future studies to clarify the relationship between self-congruity and loyalty.

Future studies can continue to explore destination loyalty in recreation farms or other destinations with a focus on the revisit market segment. Because the results of the study indicate that visit experience may moderate the relationship between self-congruity and destination loyalty, future research may adopt visit experience as a moderator in exploring the influence of visit experience. On the other hand, innovation (Litvin, Goh, & Goldsmith, 2001), knowledge (Sirgy & Su, 2000), need for variety (Castro et al., 2007), previous experience (Beerli & Martín, 2004), and involvement (Beerli et al., 2007) can also be added to discuss the mechanism from destination image to destination loyalty. Finally, the role of cognitive and affective factors needs to be empirically tested in different destinations (Morais & Lin, 2010).

Acknowledgment

The authors thank the Chung-Cheng Agriculture Science & Social Welfare Foundation, Taiwan, for financially supporting this research under Contract No. 99-09. Ted Knoy's editorial assitance is appreciated.

References

Aaker, J. L. (1997). Dimensions of brand personality. *Journal of Marketing Research, 34*(3), 347–356.

Anderson, J. C., & Gerbing, D. W. (1988). Structural equation modeling in practice: A review and recommended two-step approach. *Psychological Bulletin, 103*(3), 411–423.

Bagozzi, R. P., & Yi, Y. (1988). On the evaluation of structural equation models. *Journal of the Academy of Marketing Science, 16*(1), 76–94.

Baloglu, S., & McCleary, K. W. (1999). A model of destination image formation. *Annals of Tourism Research, 26*(4), 868–897.

Bao, Y., Bao, Y., & Sheng, S. (2011). Motivating purchase of private brands: Effects of store image, product signatureness, and quality variation. *Journal of Business Research, 64*(2), 220–226.

Beerli, A., & Martín, J. D. (2004). Factors influencing destination image. *Annals of Tourism Research, 31*(3), 657–681.

Beerli, A., Meneses, G. D., & Gil, S. M. (2007). Self-congruity and destination choice. *Annals of Tourism Research, 34*(3), 571–587.

Bentler, P. M., & Wu, E. J. C. (1993). *EQS/Windows user's guide.* Los Angeles, CA: BMDP Statistical Software.

Bigne, J. E., Sanchez, M. I., & Sanchez, J. (2001). Tourism image, evaluation variables and after purchase behavior: Interrelationship. *Tourism Management, 22*(6), 607–616.

Birgit, L. (2001). Image segmentation: The case of a tourism destination. *Journal of Service Marketing, 15*(1), 49–66.

Castro, C. B., Armario, E. M., & Ruiz, D. M. (2007). The influence of market heterogeneity on the relationship between a destination's image and tourists' future behaviour. *Tourism Management, 28*(1), 175–187.

Chen, C. F., & Tsai, D. (2007). How destination image and evaluative factors affect behavioral intentions? *Tourism Management, 28*(4), 1115–1122.

Chi, C. G.-Q., & Qu, H. (2008). Examining the structural relationships of destination image, tourist satisfaction and destination loyalty: An integrated approach. *Tourism Management, 29* (4), 624–636.

Crompton, J. L. (1979). Motivations for pleasure vacation. *Annals of Tourism Research, 6*(4), 408–424.

Dick, A. S., & Basu, K. (1994). Customer loyalty: Toward an integrated conceptual framework. *Journal of the Academy of Marketing Science, 22*(2), 99–113.

Ekinci, Y. (2003). From destination image to destination branding: An emerging area of research. *E-Review of Tourism Research, 1*(2), 1–4.

Ekinci, Y., & Hosany, S. (2006). Destination personality: An application of brand personality to tourism destinations. *Journal of Travel Research, 45*(2), 127–139.

Ekinci, Y., Sirakaya-Turk, E., & Baloglu, S. (2007). Host image and destination personality. *Tourism Analysis, 12*(5–6), 433–446.

Fakeye, P. C., & Crompton, J. L. (1991). Image differences between prospective, first-time, repeat visitors to the lower Rio Grande Valley. *Journal of Travel Research, 30*(2), 10–16.

Fornell, C., & Larcker, D. (1981). Evaluating structure equations models with unobservable variables and measurement error. *Journal of Marketing Research, 18*(1), 39–50.

Freling, T. H., Crosno, J. L., & Henard, D. H. (2011). Brand personality appeal: Conceptualization and empirical validation. *Journal of the Academy of Marketing Science, 39*(3), 392–406.

Freling, T. H., & Forbes, L. P. (2005). An examination of brand personality through methodological triangulation. *Brand Management, 13*(2), 148–162.

Gartner, W. C. (1993). Image formation process. *Journal of Travel & Tourism Marketing, 2*(2/3), 191–215.

Geuens, M., Weijters, B., & Wulf, K. D. (2009). A new measure of brand personality. *International Journal of Research in Marketing, 26*(2), 97–107.

Goh, H., & Litvin, S. (2000). *Destination preference and self-congruity*. Paper presented at the annual conference of Travel and Tourism Research Association, Burbank, CA, June, 2000.

Govers, R., Go, F. M., & Kumar, K. (2007). Promoting tourism destination image. *Journal of Travel Research, 46*(1), 15–23.

Helgeson, J. G., & Supphellen, M. (2004). A conceptual and measurement comparison of self-congruity and brand personality: The impact of socially desirable responding. *International Journal of Market Research, 46*(2), 205–233.

Hoeffler, S., & Keller, K. L. (2003). The marketing advantage of strong brands. *Journal of Brand Management, 10*(6), 421–445.

Homburg, C., Grozdanovic, M., & Klarmann, M. (2007). Responsiveness to customers and competitors: The role of affective and cognitive organizational systems. *Journal of Marketing, 71*(3), 18–38.

Hosany, S., Ekinci, Y., & Uysal, M. (2006). Destination image and destination personality: An application of branding theories to tourism places. *Journal of Business Research, 59*(5), 638–642.

Hung, K., & Petrick, J. F. (2011). The role of self- and functional congruity in cruising intentions. *Journal of Travel Research, 50*(1), 100–112.

Johar, G. V., Sengupta, J., & Aaker, J. L. (2005). Two roads to updating brand personality impressions: Trait versus evaluative inferencing. *Journal of Marketing Research, 42*(4), 458–469.

Kastenholz, E. (2004). Assessment and role of destination-self-congruity. *Annals of Tourism Research, 31*(3), 719–723.

Kneesel, E., Baloglu, S., & Millar, M. (2010). Gaming destination images: Implications for branding. *Journal of Travel Research, 49*(1), 68–78.

Kressmann, F., Sirgy, M. J., Herrmann, A., Huber, F., Huber, S., & Lee, D.-J. (2006). Direct and indirect effects of self-image congruence on brand loyalty. *Journal of Business Research, 59*(9), 955–964.

Leisen, B. (2001). Image segmentation: The case of a tourism destination. *Journal of Services Marketing, 15*(1), 49–66.

Lin, C. H., Morais, D. B., Kerstetter, D. L., & Hou, J. S. (2007). Examining the role of cognitive and affective image in predicting choice across natural, developed, and theme-park destinations. *Journal of Travel Research, 46*(2), 183–194.

Litvin, S. W., & Goh, H. K. (2002). Self-image congruity: A valid tourism theory? *Tourism Management, 23*(1), 81–83.

Litvin, S. W., Goh, H. K., & Goldsmith, R. E. (2001). Travel innovativeness and self-image congruity. *Journal of Travel and Tourism Marketing, 10*(4), 33–45.

Morais, D. B., & Lin, C. H. (2010). Why do first-time and repeat visitors patronize a destination? *Journal of Travel and Tourism Marketing, 27*(2), 193–210.

Morgan, N., & Pritchard, A. (2002). Contextualizing destination branding. In N. Morgan, A. Pritchard, & R. Pride (Eds.), *Destination branding: Creating the unique destination proposition* (pp. 11–43). Oxford, England: Butterworth-Heinemann.

Murphy, L., Benckendorff, P., & Moscardo, G. (2007). Linking travel motivation, tourist self-image and destination brand personality. *Journal of Travel and Tourism Marketing, 22*(2), 45–59.

Parameswaran, R., & Yaprak, A. (1987). A cross-national comparison of consumer research measures. *Journal of International Business Studies, 18*(1), 35–49.

Pike, S. (2002). Destination image analysis—A review of 142 papers from 1973 to 2000. *Tourism Management, 23*(5), 541–549.

Rittichainuwat, B. N., Qu, H., & Brown, T. J. (2001). Thailand's international travel image: Mostly favorable. *Cornell Hotel and Restaurant Administration Quarterly, 42*(2), 82–95.

Ross, G. F. (1993). Ideal and actual images of backpacker visitors to Northern Australia. *Journal of Travel Research, 32*(3), 54–57.

Sirgy, M. J. (1985). Using self-congruity and ideal congruity to predict purchase motivation. *Journal of Business Research, 13*(3), 195–206.

Sirgy, M. J., Grewal, D., Mangleburg, T. F., Park, J., Chon, K., Claiborne, C. B., . . ., Berkman, H. (1997). Assessing the predictive validity of two methods of measuring self image congruence. *Journal of the Academy of Marketing Science, 25*(3), 229–241.

Sirgy, M. J., Lee, D.-J., Johar, J. S., & Tidwell, J. (2008). Effect of self-congruity with sponsorship on brand loyalty. *Journal of Business Research, 61*(10), 1091–1097.

Sirgy, M. J., & Su, C. (2000). Destination image, self-congruity, and travel behavior: Toward an integrative model. *Journal of Travel Research, 38*(4), 340–352.

Sobel, M. E. (1982). Asymptotic confidence intervals for indirect effects in structural equation models. In S. Leinhart (Ed.), *Sociological methodology* (pp. 290–312). San Francisco, CA: Jossey-Bass.

Sung, Y., & Kim, J. (2010). Effects of brand personality on brand trust and brand affect. *Psychology and Marketing, 27*(7), 639–661.

Swaminathan, V., Stilley, K. M., & Ahluwalia, R. (2009). When brand personality matters: The moderating role of attachment styles. *Journal of Consumer Research, 35*(6), 985–1002.

Taiwan Council of Agriculture. (2010). 發展休閒農業 [Developing recreation farming]. Retrieved from http://www.coa.gov.tw/view.php?catid=19201

Taiwanese Recreation Farming Development Association. (2010). *The introduction to Taiwanese Recreation Farming Development Association.* Retrieved from http://www.taiwan-farming.org.tw/

Tasci, A. D. A. (2009). Social distance: The missing link in the loop of movies, destination image, and tourist behavior? *Journal of Travel Research, 47*(4), 494–507.

Tasci, A. D. A., & Gartner, W. C. (2007). Destination image and its functional relationships. *Journal of Travel Research, 45*(4), 413–425.

Taylor, T. B. (1998). Better loyalty measurement leads to business solutions. *Marketing News, 32* (22), 41–42.

Usakli, A., & Baloglu, S. (2011). Brand personality of tourist destinations: An application of self-congruity theory. *Tourism Management, 32*(1), 114–127.

Van Rekom, J., Jacobs, G., & Verlegh, P. W. J. (2006). Measuring and managing the essence of a brand personality. *Marketing Letters, 17*(3), 181–192.

Wu, C. H.-H., & Liang, R.-D. (2011). The relationship between white-water rafting experience formation and customer reaction: A flow theory perspective. *Tourism Management, 32*(2), 317–325.

Zikmund, W. G. (2003). *Business research methods* (7th ed.). Mason, OH: South-Western Publishing.

Selection of Outbound Package Tours: The Case of Senior Citizens in Hong Kong

选择出境旅行团—以香港长者为例

LOUISA YEE-SUM LEE
HENRY TSAI
NELSON K. F. TSANG
ADA S. Y. LO

Strong evidence points to an increasing number of senior citizens in the outbound travel market in Hong Kong. However, only a limited number of travel agencies in Hong Kong have paid attention to this potential market. This research investigates Hong Kong senior citizens' perceptions of the importance of the criteria used to select from the outbound package tours currently offered in the market and of the performance of these attributes. Importance–performance analysis (IPA) was carried out to analyze the data collected and categorize them into the four quadrants of the IPA grid. The results indicate the high mobility of senior citizens in Hong Kong and that they tend to join outbound package tours when traveling abroad. With regard to the provision of outbound package tours, they are generally satisfied with the performance of existing travel agencies, although some areas for improvement are noted. The findings also lend support to the high potential that exists in the senior citizen travel market and to the need for travel agencies to put extra effort into this niche market. Building upon previous literatures focusing only on selection criteria of group package tours, our study contributes further to the body of knowledge on seniors' travel decision making and the perception gap between them and the service providers. Recommendations to travel agencies regarding how to capture this market segment more effectively are also offered.

有力证据显示香港的出境旅游市场中长者的数目不断增加。然而，只有少数香港旅行社关注这一潜在市场。以目前市场上已有的出境旅行团为基础，本研究旨在探讨香港长者对选择旅行团的准则的重要性跟绩效的看法。作者采用重要性-绩效分析法（IPA）对所得数据进行分析，并在IPA方格上按结果分为四个象

Louisa Yee-Sum Lee is a research student in the School of Hotel and Tourism Management at The Hong Kong Polytechnic University, Kowloon, Hong Kong, China.

Henry Tsai is Associate Professor in the School of Hotel and Tourism Management at The Hong Kong Polytechnic University, Kowloon, Hong Kong, China.

Nelson K. F. Tsang is Assistant Professor in the School of Hotel and Tourism Management at The Hong Kong Polytechnic University, Kowloon, Hong Kong, China.

Ada S. Y. Lo is Assistant Professor in the School of Hotel and Tourism Management at The Hong Kong Polytechnic University, Kowloon, Hong Kong, China.

限。结果发现香港长者流动性高，于出外旅游时往往会参加旅行团。他们普遍满意现有旅行社的表现，但亦指出了一些要改进的地方。调查结果还确认了长者旅游市场的高潜力，旅行社需要投放更多资源到这利基市场。在着眼于旅行团的选择标准的文献基础上，本研究进一步讨论长者的旅游决策行为和他们跟服务提供者之间的认知差距，还为旅行社在如何更有效地抓紧这一细分市场的商机方面提供建议。

关键词: 长者，出境旅行团，重要性-绩效分析，香港

Introduction

Consumers aged 55 and above represent one of the fastest growing segments in the population (Shoemaker, 1989), and people aged 60 and above are expected to account for 22% of the world's population by 2050, compared to only 10% in 2000 (United Nations, 2002). The growing population of senior citizens not only contributes significantly to the travel and tourism market (Javalgi, Thomas, & Rao, 1992) in terms of visitor arrivals but is also responsible for a large share of holiday spending. The number of international travelers aged 60 and above surpassed 593 million in 1999 and is estimated to exceed 2 billion by 2050 (World Tourism Organization, 2001). Hong Kong has also witnessed a rapid growth in its population aged 60 and above, a 5.1% annual rate increase during the period 1961–2006 (Census & Statistics Department, 2006a). *The Epoch Times* (2012) reported that Hong Kongers have the longest average life expectancy in the world (females, 86.7 years old and males, 80.5). At a current retirement age of 60 to 65 in practice, retirees in Hong Kong have about 15 to 25 years of retirement. In other words, senior citizens represent a promising market for the travel industry.

Hong Kong's outbound tourism development was flourishing, recording approximately 82 million person-time traveling in 2008 and accounting for a 1.5% increase compared with 2007 (Hong Kong Tourism Board, 2009). Part of this increase in outbound travel could be due to senior citizens. A survey of millionaires in Hong Kong in 2008 showed that 27% of the millionaires were retirees, followed by housewives (15%), professionals (15%), businessmen (13%), and executives (10%; *Metro Daily*, 2009a). The survey result implies that, in Hong Kong, compared to other demographic groups, senior citizens generally possess more discretionary income. This could mean that, in terms of contributing to the outbound travel market, senior citizens have great potential, a fact that was noted by the chief executive officer (CEO) of a leading travel agency specializing in outbound tours in Hong Kong (*Metro Daily*, 2009b). Furthermore, in terms of the number of travelers to Guangdong Province, Macao, and other places during the 12 months before the 2006 enumeration, retirees outnumbered other groups among the economically inactive aged 16 and above, such as homemakers and students (Census & Statistics Department, 2006b). These statistics indicate the potential of senior citizen travelers and support the quest to study their travel needs. They not only have plenty of time but are also likely to have a looser budget for traveling.

Despite the promising market size and potential of senior citizen travelers, only a limited number of outbound package tours targeting senior citizens are offered in Hong Kong. Of the 1,499 travel agencies operating in Hong Kong (Travel Industry Council of Hong Kong, 2009), only a small number offer short-haul outbound tours for senior citizens, not to mention long-haul or other types of tours. This group of travelers has long been overlooked. Patterson (1996) noted that senior citizens prefer to travel on package tours; therefore, the travel industry ought to value this segment and seek to better understand the needs of the senior market. Although there have been a number of studies examining issues such as purchasing decisions on group package tours (e.g., Lo & Lam, 2004; K. C. Wang, Chen, & Chou, 2007) and factors that influence the choice of a travel agency (e.g., Heung & Chu, 2000), to the best of our knowledge, existing literature on the perception gap between travel agency and senior tourists in terms of group package tour selection criteria is scarce. Therefore, the purpose of this study is not only to examine Hong Kong senior citizens' perceptions of the importance of the selection criteria related to the outbound package tours currently offered in the market but also to assess their perceptions of the performance of these attributes using the importance–performance analysis (IPA) technique. By crystallizing the perception gaps, this study provides travel agencies with concrete means to help improve the quality of life for seniors through package offers that really meet their needs and wants.

Literature Review

The size and spending power of the senior market is growing. The literature and theories related to senior tourism are well explored in developed societies and Western cultures. However, little is known about the booming senior travel market in Oriental cultures, particularly in Hong Kong. There is no compelling reason to generalize senior travelers' behaviors from studies conducted in Western cultures, and this study broadens existing senior tourism literature from the perspective of Oriental senior travelers. In addition, an array of senior tourism literature has been put forth, including literature on senior travelers' behaviors (e.g., S. C. Chen & Gassner, 2012; Huang & Tsai, 2003) and their motivations (e.g., Hsu, Cai, & Wong, 2007). Knowledge regarding the perception gap between travel agencies and senior travelers is, however, limited. This study provides empirical evidence to further explore seniors as an eye-catching segment. We review studies related to seniors' travel-related motivations, barriers, and behaviors. To highlight the uniqueness of the Hong Kong senior segment, Chinese cultural influences on their travel behavior are also discussed.

Motivations for and Barriers to Senior Citizen Travel

Motivations for senior citizens to travel include socializing with friends and family, physical exercise, escaping from daily routine, and relaxation (B. D. Lee, 2005). Y. Wang (2005) pointed out that people reaching the mature stage of life are more preoccupied with self-utilization. Senior citizens look for self-fulfilling activities and are motivated to explore the world as long as their physical abilities allow them to do so. Milman (1998) observed a positive association between senior citizens' level of happiness and their participation in leisure activities on trips, such as city sightseeing, visiting historical places, and shopping. Participating in more trip-related leisure activities contributes to a positive change in their psychological well-being. Hsu et al. (2007) interviewed Chinese senior travelers, highlighting that rewarding past hardships, improving physical and mental well-being, and discovering the country's changes were also driving forces for travel. Furthermore, nostalgia-seeking was a strong motive for Chinese seniors. A Chinese proverb "returning home in glory," describing those people who left home at a young age and returned wealthy as seniors, shows that Chinese have strong emotional attachments and long to visit their ancestral homes or birthplaces. Many local senior citizens migrated to Hong Kong since 1949 due to the rapid economic growth and stable social conditions (Tse, Belk, & Zhou, 1989). Thus, traveling to one's hometown is one of the travel motives for Chinese seniors who have migrated.

On the other hand, the key constraints preventing senior citizens from traveling include poor health, insufficient money, disability, lack of a companion to travel with, and the perception that they are too old to travel (S. H. Lee & Tideswell, 2005). Other considerations are discouragement from family members and feeling guilty about traveling at their senior age. Patterson (1996) classified three constraints on senior citizens traveling: travelers' personal problems, such as health, age, and family responsibilities; travel providers' responsibilities, including cost and insufficient provision of information; and the government's travel policies, including external factors such as security concerns and environmental barriers. With heightening fears about terrorist attacks and crime rates, perceived safety is of particular importance to senior travelers (Blazey, 1992).

Muller and O'Cass (2001) claimed that the perceived risks of traveling may affect a person's decision to travel or even override his or her personal travel motives. Such perceived risks include being ill on holidays, not getting value for money, potential problems occurring with travel arrangements, the prolonged duration of holidays, and not being personally satisfied. The level of risk is likely to correlate positively with the tourist's age (Lindqvist & Bjork, 2000). All in all, time constraints, cost, lack of interest, poor health, safety, and security are key barriers for senior citizens who are considering traveling abroad. The motivations and barriers are depicted in Figure 1 and some of these were considered for inclusion in the questionnaire survey to identify the perception gap between senior citizens and travel agencies in Hong Kong.

Senior Citizens' Selection of All-Inclusive Package Tours

Senior citizen travelers, compared to their non-senior counterparts, prefer joining outbound package tours (Javalgi et al., 1992) and rely heavily on travel agencies to make their travel arrangements by taking advantage of all-inclusive package tours (Blazey, 1992; B. D. Lee, 2005). An all-inclusive package tour is defined as a trip planned and paid for by an all-inclusive and in-advance payment, covering

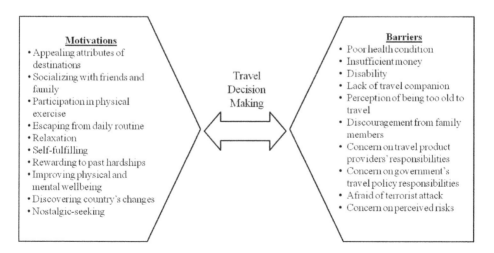

Figure 1. Motivations and barriers for Chinese senior travelers. (Summarized from Blazey, 1992; Hsu et al., 2007; Lee, 2005; Lee & Tideswell, 2005; Muller & O'Cass, 2001; Patterson, 1996; Wang, 2005)

commercial transportation, accommodations, meals, and sightseeing (Heung & Chu, 2000; Wong & Lau, 2001). These all-inclusive tour packages provide travelers with increased convenience and value, a reduced possibility of hassles and surprises, an increased sense of security and safety, social benefits of traveling with a group of other people, and the convenience of being escorted throughout the trip (Burke & Resnick, 2000; de Souto, 1985; Lo & Lam, 2004). Taking value for money into consideration, participating in a package tour is probably the most effective and rational means of achieving a travel goal, because it allows a traveler to visit the largest number of interesting sites and attractions on a restricted time schedule (Enoch, 1996; Heung & Chu, 2000). Group package tourists are also assured that the itinerary will be followed and that the products and services listed in the printed tour brochure will be provided.

For senior citizens, convenience is a primary reason for deciding whether or not to join package tours (Patterson, 1996). They may find the physical requirements of independent travel quite inconvenient and demanding; for instance, purchasing tickets, handling baggage, and walking long distances on their own. In addition, senior citizens are, compared to their non-senior counterparts, more price sensitive (Javalgi et al., 1992). A package tour is usually much less expensive because a travel agency can take advantage of bulk purchases on hotel accommodations, meals, and transportation at discounted group rates (Enoch, 1996). Therefore, joining a package tour appears to be a better option for senior citizens to travel.

From the senior traveler's perspective, safety and security are great benefits of joining package tours. All-inclusive package tours are worry-free because all elements, such as travel, accommodations, and meals, are preplanned (Patterson, 1996). Group tourists can carry comparatively less foreign currency and worry less about tipping. Enoch (1996) also pointed out that joining a package tour offers a sense of safety when traveling to destinations with a different culture, dubious hygiene conditions, and unreliable transportation. Therefore, the stress commonly associated with individual travel can be reduced. In addition, most Hong Kong tourists generally do not search for information about their destinations before joining tours; instead, they rely heavily on the travel agency (Wong & Lau, 2001). Being unfamiliar with foreign languages and information search technology, senior citizen travelers tend to join package tours as organized mass tourists. It is convenient for them to leave such tasks to professional travel agencies. Lacking travel companions is likely another consideration of senior citizens (Patterson, 1996). They choose to join group tours to socialize, meet people, and develop friendships (Shoemaker, 2000).

Mode of Outbound Travel Preferred by Senior Citizens

Over 60% of senior citizens aged 55 or above prefer traveling by automobile, followed by plane (Javalgi et al., 1992). The automobile is a comparatively more flexible and less expensive mode of travel. Nevertheless, Javalgi et al.'s (1992) study was conducted in the U.S. context, and the findings may not be applicable to other parts of the world. In places such as Hong Kong, outbound travel by automobile may be less desirable. In addition, a higher percentage of senior citizens travel by plane than their non-senior counterparts, most likely due to the speed and convenience of air travel.

The cruise ship industry has seen an annual growth rate of 8.4% since 1980, representing one of the fastest growing segments in the tourism sector (Goeldner &

Ritchie, 2003) and has become popular among senior citizens. A cruise ship offers a wide range of leisure and entertainment options, such as gaming and musical performances, as well as shopping and other recreational services and facilities. It allows greater flexibility in terms of traveling time, and senior citizens can enjoy their trip at their own pace (Patterson, 1996). Hong Kong residents enjoy traveling by cruise ship because it provides a one-stop platform for accommodations, food and beverages, and entertainment (Qu & Wong, 1999), and senior citizens with time and a discretionary budget could be a revenue generator for the cruise industry.

Travel Characteristics of Senior Citizens

Senior citizens are more experienced travelers and feel comfortable about continuing to travel (Lohmann & Danielsson, 2001). Though Hong Kong residents enjoy outbound travel (Chan, David, Fong, & Wong, 2005), little is known about the travel characteristics of senior citizens. A number of studies have reported senior citizens' preferences in terms of holiday destinations and activities (e.g., Littrell, Paige, & Song, 2004; Zimmer, Brayley, & Searle, 1995). Muller and O'Cass (2001) discovered that, similar to their non-senior counterparts, senior citizens use travel as a means of enjoying life and gaining a sense of accomplishment. Their desired destinations are locations with natural beauty, photo safaris, helicopter skiing, hot air ballooning, and so forth. Littrell et al. (2004) stated that senior citizen travelers are active outdoor and cultural tourists, enjoying both contemplative and active involvement with the natural environment. They appreciate the arts and culture-related activities and sampling local food, as well as hiking and eco-tours. On the other hand, Anderson and Langmeyer (1982) discussed the differences in travel characteristics between travelers younger and older than age 50. The latter population preferred traveling during nonpeak seasons because the majority of the interviewed respondents were retired. Visiting historic sites was also a preferable activity during their trips.

Females have been reported to be keen on maintaining social networks and activities via passive and expressive leisure; for example, through cultural and home-based activities (Patterson, 1996). Females, especially those aged between 55 and 59, are significantly more interested in traveling. They are more educated and have a higher level of discretionary income than their younger counterparts. The study by Patterson (1996) also showed that, compared to males, females prefer shorter tours because they are more concerned with safety issues. Furthermore, females tend to require more socializing and interaction with other people. However, females, especially those who are widowed, divorced, or do not have a partner to travel with, feel less confident about traveling alone. On the other hand, males are confident about traveling alone. Regardless of gender, Muller and O'Cass (2001) reported that senior citizens' top preference is to travel with one other person (44%), followed by traveling with a group of friends only (20%) or with friends and family together (14%). Hence, senior citizens prefer traveling with a small group of companions.

In 1996, as cited in Shoemaker (2000), 10,000 randomly selected U.S. households were interviewed for a survey on the travel expenditure of various age groups. In terms of the amount of average household income spent on travel, respondents (a) under 35 spent $3,024 (5.8% of household income); (b) aged 35–44 spent $2,712 (4.8% of household income); (c) aged 45–54 spent $3,213 (5.5% of household income), and (d) over 65 spent $3,192 (10.8% of household income). Among all of the interviewees, the group aged between 55 and 64 years of age spent an average of $3,314 (7.1% of their average household income) on travel in 1996. The figures showed that members of the mature market spent relatively more on travel, despite having lower household incomes.

Chinese Cultural Influences on Senior Travelers' Behavior

Numerous researchers conceive that culture does color travelers' behavior (e.g., Ahmed & Krohn, 1992; Pizam & Jeong, 1996; Reimer, 1990; Richardson & Crompton, 1988; Wong & Lau, 2001; Yavas, 1987), as well as motivating people to undertake travel (e.g., Kim & Chalip, 2004; Zhang & Lam, 1999). Hofstede (1983) defined *culture* as a "collective mental programming that we share with other members of our nation, region, or group but not with members of other nations, regions, or groups" (p. 76), which has been widely adopted by cultural studies. Hofstede (1980, 1993) proposed five national culture dimensions: power distance, collectivism/individualism, uncertainty avoidance, long-term/short-term orientation, and masculinity/feminism. Chinese people have a strong long-term orientation and collectivism culture, characterized by seeking harmony and being more group oriented. Bond's (1986) Chinese Culture Connection study echoed Hofstede's viewpoint, asserting the vigorous values of collectivism and compassion rooted in Chinese culture. N. K. F. Tsang (2011) surveyed approximately 800 Hong Kong hospitality and tourism employees, wherein "harmony with others" was one of the top five most influential values out of 32 Chinese cultural values. Therefore, Hong Kong travelers who favor traveling in groups and joining packaged tours can be plausibly interpreted by the Chinese cultural characteristics of seeking comfort and association and preferring a familiar atmosphere to unfamiliar destinations (Kaynak & Kucukemiroglu, 1993; Mok & Armstrong, 1995; Plog, 2001).

Another ideology rooted in Chinese traditions is the high value placed on family (E. W. K. Tsang, 2001; Xing, 1995). Seniors are generally believed to have plenty of time to travel or participate in leisure activities. In the Chinese cultural context, Chinese seniors venerate intergenerational reciprocity. Hsu et al. (2007) pointed out that Chinese seniors' time is constrained by family issues, such as taking caring of their spouses and families of their children, because being with children is a reflection of family unity. They place their housework as a first priority, despite having strong interests in traveling. This may be due to the psychological benefits in committing to their offspring and grandchildren and dependence on their children for financial support (Chen and Silverstein, 2000; Luborsky and McMullen, 1999). Rapid social and economic development may also change the seniors' traditional values due to the influence of modern Western cultures (Tan, 1981). However, some cultural values are transmitted across time, which is difficult to change (Hofstede & Bond, 1988). These Chinese cultural values are, therefore, perceived as influential with regard to Chinese senior travelers' behaviors.

Methodology

In this study, a questionnaire survey was employed to achieve the research objectives of assessing the perceived importance and performance of the attributes related to outbound package tour selection from senior citizens' perspectives in Hong Kong. In our study, a *senior citizen* is defined as aged 55 years or older, because this is the normal retirement age for civil servants in Hong Kong.

Instrument Design

The items in the survey instrument that measured the outbound package tour selection criteria were derived from the literature on travel motivation, barriers, and behaviors and personal conversations with CEOs of travel agencies in Hong Kong (e.g., Andereck, 2005; Berry, 1995; Heung & Chu, 2000; Hruschka & Mazanec, 1990; Hsieh, Pan, & Setiono, 2004; Javalgi et al., 1992; Lo & Lam, 2004; Ng, Cassidy, & Brown, 2006; Patterson, 1996). A list of 24 attributes related to outbound package tour selection was compiled. Examples of the attributes include variety of tours, destination selection, safety and security, value for money, additional services, service quality, knowledgeable travel agency, corporate image, brand identity, duration, group size, and extent of physically challenging activities. Back-translation was performed to derive a bilingual version of the survey because not all senior citizens are English literate.

The questionnaire started with two screening questions in order to include only those interviewees who were Hong Kong residents aged 55 years or older and had previously joined an outbound package tour organized by a registered Hong Kong travel agency. The second section was designed to assess their perceptions of outbound package tours. Base on the 24 attributes, the target respondents rated their perceptions of the importance and performance, respectively, of the attributes related to outbound package tours on a Likert-type scale ranging from 1 to 5, where 1 indicated *least important* (for the importance rating) or *worst performing* (for the performance rating) and 5 indicated *most important* (for the importance rating) or *best performing* (for the performance rating).

Demographic information of the respondents, including gender, age range, range of monthly household income, and travel behaviors, was collected in the third section. Prior to the mass surveys, a pilot test was conducted with eight Hong Kong senior citizens over 55 years old to minimize ambiguity and ensure the clarity of the questionnaire. Some wording was rephrased and sentences were modified after the pilot test.

Sampling and Data Collection

The survey was carried out in the afternoon, from 12 p.m. to 4 p.m., on 10 randomly selected days in July 2009. The days included both weekdays and weekends. Three locations—Kowloon Bay, Diamond Hill, and Central—were chosen for distribution of the questionnaire. Kowloon Bay and Diamond Hill are residential areas, and it was easy to approach eligible respondents in a relaxed manner. Central was chosen in order to collect more diverse data and information, because people working or living in Central tend to have higher disposable incomes. Convenience sampling was adopted. Potential respondents were approached when they came out of travel agencies, because this could be an indication that they had the intention of traveling abroad. If a selected respondent was not willing to participate in our survey or did not belong to the targeted respondent group, the next immediate respondent was invited to be interviewed. Due to the difficulty encountered in approaching senior citizens using the street intercept method, snowball sampling was also employed.

Data Analysis

The data collected were analyzed in a series of steps, and the whole data analysis process was performed using the IBM Statistical Package for the Social Sciences (SPSS) software. The data were initially screened for missing values or invalid data entries; no specific outliers were present. Descriptive statistics were calculated and a ranking of the individual attributes was performed. We then performed IPA to identify the gap between the respondents' perceptions of the (a) importance and (b) performance of the attributes related to outbound package tour selection. The mean score of each attribute was plotted in an IPA grid, which was divided into four quadrants, namely, "concentrate here," "keep up the good work," "low priority," and "possible overkill." Through the IPA analysis, management actions or applications can be suggested for the various attributes in the four quadrants.

Results and Discussion

Respondents' Demographic Profile

Table 1 presents the demographic profile of the respondents. Two hundred Hong Kong senior citizens were interviewed, and their questionnaires were deemed valid. Males accounted for 40% of the respondents and females 60%. The majority of respondents (64%) were between 55 and 60, 29% were 61 to 65, and 7% were 66 years old or older. Of the respondents, nearly 68% were married with children, 15% were married with no children, 13.5% were single, and 4% stated that their marital status was "other." In terms of education, the majority of the respondents (43.7%) had received a secondary-level education, 28% had received a primary-level education or below, about 20% had a postsecondary or college education, and 8.5% had a university or a postgraduate degree. Over 50% of the respondents had a monthly household income of more than HK$20,000 and 26.5% had an income of between HK$10,000 and HK$19,999.

Travel Characteristics of Senior Citizens

The travel characteristics of the respondents are given in Table 2. This table shows that 85% of the respondents had traveled abroad within the 12-month period prior to taking the survey and that 70% generally joined outbound package tours when traveling abroad, which echoes Patterson's (1996) study. Their preferred mode of transportation was plane (33.5%), followed by cruise (30%), coach (21%), and rail (13.5%). The survey revealed that 40% of the respondents traveled abroad by joining outbound package tours every one to 2 years, and about one fourth of the respondents traveled every 7–11 months. Including tour fees and self-expenditures, nearly 40% of the respondents were willing to spend between HK$5,001 and HK$15,000, 22% HK$5,000 or below, and 22.9% between HK$15,001 and HK$25,000. Over half of the respondents (53%) mentioned that they would almost always join package tours when traveling abroad (8 to 10 out of 10 outbound travels).

Importance and Performance Attribute Ranking

Table 3 presents the mean scores for the respondents' perceptions of the importance and performance of the 24 attributes related to outbound package tours in descending order. Generally speaking, the importance ratings of the attributes, which ranged from 3.56 to 4.51, were generally higher than those of the performance attributes, which ranged from 2.55 to 3.77.

Table 1. Demographic Information of Respondents ($n = 200$).

	Frequency	Percentage
Gender		
Male	80	40
Female	120	60
Age group		
55–60	128	64
61–65	58	29
66 or older	14	7
Marital status		
Married with children	135	67.5
Married without children	30	15
Single	27	13.5
Other	8	4
Education level		
Primary level or below	56	28
Secondary level	87	43.7
Postsecondary level or college	40	20.1
Degree or postgraduate	17	8.5
Monthly household income		
No income	14	7.1
Below HK$10,000	22	11.2
HK$10,000–HK$19,999	53	26.5
HK$20,000–HK$29,999	73	36.5
HK$30,000 or above	38	19.3

The top three importance rankings were safety of the destination (mean = 4.51), tour meals (mean = 4.47), and quality of hotel or accommodations (mean = 4.38), whereas the top three performance rankings were safety of the destination (mean = 3.77), familiarity with the destination (mean = 3.62), and familiarity with the language of the destination (mean = 3.56). On the other hand, the least important attributes were recommendation from a travel expert (mean = 3.56), incentives (mean = 3.61), and advertising (mean = 3.61), and the least performing attributes were incentives (mean = 2.55), price of activities requiring an extra payment (mean = 2.58), and extent of activities requiring an extra payment (mean = 2.82).

Not surprisingly, safety of the destination was ranked as the most important attribute. Furthermore, it was also perceived as the best performing attribute. In Lo and Lam's study (2004) on Hong Kong residents' selection criteria for all-inclusive outbound package tours, personal safety was also identified as the most important selection criterion. Travel agencies in Hong Kong should be commended for delivering the attribute that is perceived not only by senior citizens but residents of all age groups as being the most important when choosing outbound package tours. Our study also echoes Enoch's (1996) finding that joining a package tour was considered a relatively safe way to travel to different countries with different cultures, unreliable transportation, and dubious standards of hygiene. The results also were similar to the research by Jang and Wu (2006), who reported that Taiwanese seniors signify cleanliness and safety

Table 2. Travel Characteristics ($n = 200$).

	Frequency	Percentage
Traveled abroad within the past 12 months		
Yes	170	85
No	30	15
Joined an outbound package tour when traveling		
Yes	135	67.5
No	65	32.5
Favorite mode of transportation		
Airplane	67	33.5
Cruise	60	30
Coach	42	21
Rail	31	13.5
Average frequency of joining outbound package tours		
Every 1–6 months	39	5
Every 7–11 months	49	24.5
Every 1–2 years	80	40
Less than every 2 years	32	16
Budget for next outbound package tour		
(including tour fee and self-expenditure)		
HK$5,000 or below	23	22
HK$5,001–HK$15,000	40	38.2
HK$15,001–HK$25,000	24	22.9
HK$25,001–HK$35,000	6	5.8
HK$35,001 or above	12	11.6
Numbers of trips taken on package tours		
(out of 10 outbound travels)		
1–4	29	19.5
5–7	41	27.5
8–10	79	53

as key considerations. Similar to the results of Lo and Lam (2004), the quality of accommodations and meals was among the top five most important attributes in selecting all-inclusive package tours. The finding was somewhat different for Asian travelers of all ages, who viewed cost as the most critical attribute (e.g., Yuan & McDonald, 1990; Zhang & Lam, 1999). Nevertheless, other top-ranked important attributes, such as tour meals, quality of hotel or accommodations, extent of activities requiring an extra payment, price of activities requiring an extra payment, and price of tour were all perceived to be among the worst performing attributes. On the other hand, some less important attributes, such as recommendation from a travel expert, advertising, and word of mouth, were perceived as performing well and having a great influence on the senior citizens' selection of an outbound package tour.

Respondents considered recommendation from a travel expert the least important attribute, probably due to common advertising practices adopted by travel agencies in Hong Kong. Travel experts or celebrities are sometimes hired to write advertorials or to endorse travel agencies and, as a result, such recommendations may not truly reflect the

Table 3. Ranking of Perceived Importance of Joining Outbound Package Tour and Current Performance of Travel Agency (Sorted by Importance Ranking).

Perceived Importance Mean Score (Ranking)	Attribute	Current Performance Mean Score (Ranking)
4.51 (1st)	Safety of the destination	3.77 (1st)
4.47 (2nd)	Tour meals	2.91 (21st)
4.38 (3rd)	Quality of hotel or accommodations	3.14 (14th)
4.36 (4th)	Extent of activities requiring an extra payment	2.82 (22nd)
4.32 (5th)	Price of activities requiring an extra payment	2.58 (23rd)
4.24 (6th)	Price of tour	2.99 (19th)
4.19 (7th)	Itinerary	3.19 (9th)
4.18 (8th)	Value for money	3.09 (16th)
4.16 (9th)	Duration of tour	3.13 (15th)
4.13 (10th)	Size of tour group	3.09 (17th)
4.08 (11th)	Extent of physically challenging activities	3.17 (11th)
4.04 (12th)	Choice of destination	3.15 (12th)
4.04 (13th)	Travel agency's reputation	3.42 (4th)
4.02 (14th)	Familiarity with the destination	3.62 (2nd)
3.90 (15th)	Corporate image	3.18 (10th)
3.89 (16th)	Familiarity with the language of the destination	3.56 (3rd)
3.88 (17th)	Previous personal experience	3.15 (13th)
3.85 (18th)	Quality of counseling	2.97 (20th)
3.80 (19th)	Variety	3.23 (8th)
3.78 (20th)	Knowledge level of travel agency	3.01 (18th)
3.70 (21st)	Word of mouth	3.29 (7th)
3.61 (22nd)	Advertising	3.38 (5th)
3.61 (23rd)	Incentives	2.55 (24th)
3.56 (24th)	Recommendation from a travel expert	3.37 (6th)

facts. Inconsistency was noted in previous research on travel experts' recommendations and advertising. Mok and DeFranco (1999) found that experts' comments were influential in purchase decisions because Chinese people are respectful to authority. Advertisements printed in newspapers and magazines were also a key information source for Mainland Chinese travelers (Bao, 2005). However, Hong Kongers perceived advertisements as a relatively unimportant attribute for packaged tour selection (Heung & Chu, 2000). This inconsistency may be due to the distinctive consumer cultures and advertising preferences between Mainland Chinese and Hong Kong Chinese (Tse et al., 1989). Incentives, on the other hand, was the worst performing attribute (mean = 2.55). Travel agencies generally do not offer discount coupons as a part of their marketing strategy. They may just mail discount coupons to loyal customers and the rate may not seem attractive.

Based on the above analysis of the importance and performance rankings of the attributes, it can be seen that some of the attributes perceived as important by the respondents did not perform well and vice versa. The importance ranking of some attributes—for example, extent of physically challenging activities and choice of destination—matched their individual performance rankings. It was therefore logical for us to perform IPA to allocate the various attributes into the four quadrants of the IPA grid.

Importance–Performance Analysis

In IPA, the grand mean of the overall importance dimension was 4 and that of the performance dimension was 3.13. The former represents the vertical axis (i.e., the y axis) and the latter the horizontal axis (i.e., the x axis). The importance and performance mean scores of each individual attribute were plotted on the four quadrants of the IPA grid, which is presented in Figure 2.

In the IPA grid, six attributes (value for money, price of activities requiring an extra payment, size of tour group, price of tour, tour meals, and extent of activities requiring an extra payment) were captured in quadrant A (concentrate here), where the attributes were of high importance but low performance. That is, the mean scores of these six attributes were above the grand importance mean score of 4 but below the grand performance mean of 3.13. Generally speaking, these six attributes were directly or indirectly related to the amount of money spent on a tour. Though travel agencies should work on all six attributes identified in this quadrant, particular attention should probably be paid to price of activities requiring an extra payment, tour meals, and extent of activities requiring an extra payment. Travel agencies in Hong Kong are in keen competition with each other and may sometimes engage in price wars by reducing package tour fees. The resulting effects of such practices include inferior tour quality and a reduction in the number of attractions included as part of the standard itinerary, leaving more attractions as optional and requiring an extra payment. Furthermore, travel agencies may opt to offer lower quality meals and include more customers in the group to share the fixed costs. These practices explain the poor performance of the attributes in this quadrant, which require improvement (Deng, 2007). Senior citizens' emphasis on value for money indicates that they are not only sensitive to the amount of money they pay but also want to get the most for their money.

Eight attributes were categorized into quadrant B (keep up the good work), meaning that these attributes were of both high importance and high performance. These attributes were choice of destination, safety of the destination, duration of tour, extent of physically challenging activities, travel agency's reputation, familiarity with the destination, itinerary, and quality of hotel or accommodations. Compared to the other quadrants, this quadrant received the most attributes (33%); senior citizens therefore seem to be satisfied with the current performance of travel agencies offering outbound package tours. The respondents perceived safety of the destination as the most important and best performing attribute. They were most likely to choose destinations with stable political and social environments. In addition, familiarity with the destination and the travel agency's reputation help to induce confidence. Nevertheless, it should be pointed out that quality of hotel or accommodations and duration of tour were the two attributes almost qualified for inclusion in quadrant A. Two other attributes—choice of destination and extent of physically challenging activities—were also close to being included in this quadrant. Though travel agencies

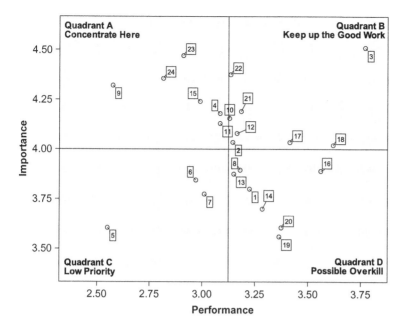

1. Variety

2. Choice of destination

3. Safety of the destination

4. Value for money

5. Incentives

6. Quality of counseling

7. Knowledge level of travel agency

8. Corporate image

9. Price of activities requiring an extra payment

10. Duration of tour

11. Size of tour group

12. Extent of physically challenging activities

13. Previous personal experience

14. Word of mouth

15. Price of tour

16. Familiarity with the language of the destination

17. Travel agency's reputation

18. Familiarity with the destination

19. Recommendation from travel expert

20. Advertising

21. Itinerary

22. Quality of hotel or accommodations

23. Meal of the tour

24. Extent of activities requiring an extra payment

Figure 2. Importance–performance grid.

in Hong Kong have generally met the requirements of senior citizens with regard to their outbound package tour selection, they should carefully reexamine their current offerings regarding the above-mentioned attributes, which relate significantly to the physical condition of senior citizens.

Quadrant C (low priority) included only three attributes: incentives, quality of counseling, and knowledge level of travel agency. All of the mean scores of the attributes in this quadrant were lower than the grand mean of both the importance and performance attributes. In other words, these attributes were of low importance and low in performance. Contrary to Hruschka and Mazanec's (1990) study, this result shows that the senior citizens in our survey did not place emphasis on the counter services provided by the staff. Most likely, the knowledge level and service quality of frontline staff were not impressive enough to affect their decisions regarding outbound package tour selection. They also thought that such counseling was not important, because they could research information related to the itinerary and price before making a decision regarding joining a package tour. Furthermore, they were not motivated by the incentives provided, because these incentives may not be attractive. Seven attributes were allocated to quadrant D (possible overkill), meaning that they were of little importance but high performance. The seven attributes were variety, corporate image, previous personal experience, word of mouth, familiarity with the language of the destination, recommendation from a travel expert, and advertising. Travel agencies targeting the mass market provide a variety of tour types, such as adventure, shopping, and sightseeing. However, senior citizens do not seem to appreciate such diverse tour experiences, possibly due to their physical constraints. Two noticeable attributes in this quadrant were recommendation from a travel expert and advertising. Senior citizens have extensive social and life experiences, and they are sophisticated enough to find relevant information, rather than relying on expert recommendations and advertising, when making tour decisions. Travel agencies may have put too much effort into expert endorsement.

Conclusion and Recommendations

The objectives of this study were to investigate Hong Kong senior citizens' perceptions of the importance and performance of the attributes related to joining an outbound package tour. Two hundred valid questionnaires were collected and the respondents were asked to rate 24 attributes derived from a literature review and personal communications with industry professionals. The importance and performance rankings were evaluated, and IPA was later employed to further categorize the importance and performance attributes into the four quadrants of the IPA grid. The results of this study showed that the majority of senior citizens travel annually and that they prefer to join a package tour when traveling abroad. When comparing the importance and performance rankings, the respondents agreed that safety of the destination is the most important attribute and that travel agencies in Hong Kong are able to meet this requirement. In addition, the IPA showed that senior citizens are generally satisfied with the performance of the attributes, but improvement is needed in value for money, price of activities requiring an extra payment, size of tour group, price of tour, tour meals, and extent of activities requiring an extra payment. Travel agencies were regarded as placing too much emphasis on some areas, such as advertising.

Our study contributes theoretically as well as practically. From a theoretical perspective, travel-related decision making is a complex process characterized by high risk and high financial cost in view of the heterogeneity characteristic of tourism product (Sirakaya & Woodside, 2005). Previous studies on group package tours (e.g., Heung & Chu, 2000; Lo & Lam, 2004; Wong & Lau, 2001) mainly focused on travelers' selection criteria, and understanding of the senior market with regard to package tour selection criteria is confined. Our study fills the void. In addition, our study ranked the attributes and applied IPA to further prioritize and foreground significant package tour selection variables, including value for money, price of tour, and size of tour group, from a vast of selection criteria from the seniors' perspectives. Financial concern was of prime importance for Hong Kong seniors in selecting outbound package tours but was not a well-performing attribute of travel agencies, because those package tour selection attributes listed in Quadrant A, concentrate here, were mostly affiliated with money. In comparison to senior citizens' travel motivations and barriers listed in Figure 1, insufficient money was only listed as an influential barrier without further indication to travel agencies on its level of importance versus performance. Assessing the importance–perception gap also suggests that travel agencies can gain insight by looking beyond generic package tour elements when designing their package tour offerings. Travel agencies in Hong Kong or other places with similar socioeconomic environments should take advantage of the results of this study. The items categorized in the four quadrants of the IPA grid offer an immediate reference for travel agencies.

A few more recommendations are offered here. First, given the great potential of the senior citizens market, travel agencies should reexamine their existing offerings and marketing strategies toward the seniors market. Understanding the need for value for money and the disregard for attributes such as travel expert endorsement and advertising, travel agencies could better allocate their resources not only to make effective and efficient use of their budgets but to benefit their potential senior citizen travelers by offering better products and the services they desire.

Second, expanding outbound package tours to Mainland China could be a viable strategy. Senior citizens in Hong Kong have a very strong sense of belonging toward Mainland China (J. Wong, personal communication, October 6, 2009) because many of their relatives still live there. They are also very familiar with Chinese customs, tradition, language, and cultural background. Therefore, China is most likely to be a popular destination for senior citizens now and in the future. Comparatively fewer barriers exist for senior citizens to travel to Mainland China. As a result, travel agencies should explore more new attractions or historical sites in China. Furthermore, travel agencies in Hong Kong operating package tours to China may attract foreign senior travelers who want to uncover the mask of China, which, in the eyes of the baby boomers in the Western world, is rather mysterious.

Third, because cruise was the second most preferred mode of travel for senior citizens, developing cruise tours would benefit both the travel agencies and senior citizens. Lohmann and Danielsson (2001) commented that cruise ships are very popular with senior citizens in Europe, and a cruise is considered suitable for the seniors market (Javalgi et al., 1992; J. Wong, personal communication, October 6, 2009). According to Javalgi et al. (1992), cruise ship travelers enjoy a wide range of onboard activities and planned stops at destinations along the way. A cruise ship provides a one-stop boarding and lodging platform, as well as entertainment. Senior citizens are freed from the worry of changing hotels and thus they encounter less physical challenges. A point to note here is the special attention given by senior citizens to the health issue and the extent of physical activities onboard.

Limitations and Directions for Future Research

A few limitations should be noted. First of all, this study was conducted using convenience sampling, which may limit the generalizability of the study's results. Secondly, the 24 attributes adopted in our study may not be comprehensive in terms of assessing the criteria for joining outbound package tours. Thirdly, the respondents in our study may have purposely given fake/false responses (e.g., indicating that their monthly household income is higher than it actually is during the face-to-face interviews), thus potentially causing social desirability bias (Crowne & Marlowe, 1960).

Future research could compare the travel destination preferences, behaviors, characteristics, and selection criteria for outbound package tours of senior citizens and non-senior citizens in Hong Kong or other places in order to further segment the two groups of consumers. In addition, an in-depth investigation into the perceptions of Hong Kong senior citizens on health tourism or cruises could lead to a better assessment of the market potential and provide practitioners with references for product development.

References

Ahmed, Z. U., & Krohn, F. B. (1992). Understanding the unique consumer behavior of Japanese tourists. *Journal of Travel & Tourism Marketing, 1*(3), 73–86.

Andereck, K. L. (2005). Evaluation of a tourist brochure. *Journal of Travel & Tourism Marketing, 18*(2), 1–13.

Anderson, B., & Langmeyer, L. (1982). The under-50 and over-50 traveler: A profile of similarities and differences. *Journal of Travel Research, 20*(4), 20–24.

Bao, J. (2005). *Going with the flow: China travel journalism in change* (PhD thesis, Creative Industries Research & Applications Centre, Queensland University of Technology). Retrieved from http://eprints.qut.edu.au/16185/1/Jiannu_Bao_Thesis.pdf

Berry, L. (1995). Relationship marketing of services—Growing interest, emerging perspectives. *Journal of Academy of Marketing Science, 23*(4), 236–245.

Blazey, M. (1992). Travel and retirement status. *Annals of Tourism Research, 19*(4), 771–783.

Bond, M. H. (1986). The social psychology of Chinese people. In M. H. Bond (Ed.), *The psychology of the Chinese people* (pp. 213–266). New York, NY: Oxford University Press.

Burke, J., & Resnick, B. (2000). *Marketing and selling the travel product* (2nd ed.). Albany, NY: Delmar.

Census & Statistics Department. (2006a). *The thematic report: Older persons*. Hong Kong, China: Government Information Services.

Census & Statistics Department. (2006b). *Thematic household survey report No. 16*. Hong Kong, China: Government Information Services.

Chan, C. M., David, P., Fong, M. S., & Wong, H. Y. (2005). *An exploratory study on the significance of outbound travelling for the older persons in Hong Kong*. Hong Kong, China: Asia–Pacific Institute of Ageing Studies, Lingnan University.

Chen, S. C., & Gassner, M. (2012). An investigation of the demographic, psychological, psychographic, and behavioral characteristics of Chinese senior leisure travelers. *Journal of China Tourism Research, 8*(2), 123–145.

Chen, X., & Silverstein, M. (2000). Intergenerational social support and the psychological well-being of older parents in China. *Research on Aging, 22*(1), 43–65.

Crowne, D. P., & Marlowe, D. (1960). A new scale of social desirability independent of psychopathology. *Journal of Consulting Psychology, 24*(4), 349–354.

Deng, W. (2007). Using a revised importance—Performance analysis approach: The case of Taiwanese hot springs tourism. *Tourism Management, 28*(5), 1274–1284.

de Souto, M. S. (1985). *Group travel operations manual*. Albany, NY: Delmar Publishers.

Enoch, Y. (1996). Contents of tour packages: A cross-cultural comparison. *Annals of Tourism Research, 23*(3), 599–616.

The Epoch Times. (2012, July 27). Hong Kong's people have longest average life expectancy of 80 plus. Retrieved from http://www.epochtimes.com/b5/12/7/27/n3644898.htm

Goeldner, C. R., & Ritchie, J. R. (2003). *Tourism: Principles, practices, philosophies*. Hoboken, NJ: John Wiley & Sons.

Heung, C. S., & Chu, R. (2000). Important factors affecting Hong Kong consumers' choice of a travel agency for all-inclusive package tours. *Journal of Travel Research, 39*(1), 52–59.

Hofstede, G. (1980). *Culture's consequences: International differences in work-related values*. London, England: Sage Publications.

Hofstede, G. (1983). The cultural relativity of organizational practices and theories [Special issue]. *Journal of International Business Studies, 14*(2), 75–89.

Hofstede, G. (1993). Cultural constraints in management theories. *The Academy of Management Executive, 7*(1), 81–94.

Hofstede, G., & Bond, M. H. (1988). The Confucian connection: From cultural roots to economic growth. *Organization Dynamics, 16*(4), 4–21.

Hong Kong Tourism Board. (2009). *A statistical review of Hong Kong tourism 2008.* Hong Kong, China: Hong Kong Tourism Board.

Hruschka, H., & Mazanec, J. (1990). Computer-assisted travel counseling. *Annals of Tourism Research, 17*(2), 208–227.

Hsieh, M. H., Pan, S. H., & Setiono R. (2004). Product-, corporate-, and country-image dimensions and purchase behavior: A multicountry analysis. *Journal of the Academy of Marketing Science, 32*(3), 251–270.

Hsu, C. H. C., Cai, L. A., & Wong, K. K. F. (2007). A model of senior tourism motivations—Anecdotes from Beijing and Shanghai. *Tourism Management, 28*(7), 1262–1273.

Huang, L., & Tsai, H. T. (2003). The study of senior traveler behavior in Taiwan. *Tourism Management, 24*(5), 561–574.

Jang, S., & Wu, C. M. E. (2006). Seniors' travel motivation and the influential factors: An examination of Taiwanese seniors. *Tourism Management, 27*(2), 306–316.

Javalgi, R., Thomas, E., & Rao, S. (1992). Consumer behavior in the U.S. pleasure travel marketplace: An analysis of senior and nonsenior travelers. *Journal of Travel Research, 31* (2), 14–19.

Kaynak, E., & Kucukemiroglu, O. (1993). Foreign vacation selection process in an Oriental culture. *Asia Pacific Journal of Marketing & Logistics, 1*(5), 21–41.

Kim, N., & Chalip, L. (2004). Why travel to the FIFA World Cup? Effects of motives, background, interest and constraints. *Tourism Management, 25*(6), 695–707.

Lee, B. D. (2005). *Motives, behaviors, and attachments: A comparative study between older travelers and younger travelers in a national scenic area* (Doctoral dissertation). Available from ProQuest Dissertations and Theses Database. (Accession Order No. 3172985)

Lee, S. H., & Tideswell, C. (2005). Understanding attitudes towards leisure travel and the constraints faced by senior Koreans. *Journal of Vacation Marketing, 11*(3), 249–263.

Lindqvist, L. J., & Bjork, P. B. (2000). Perceived safety as an important quality dimension among senior tourists. *Tourism Economics, 6*(2), 151–158.

Littrell, M., Paige, R., & Song, K. (2004). Senior travelers: Tourism activities and shopping behaviours. *Journal of Vacation Marketing, 10*(4), 348–362.

Lo, A., & Lam, T. (2004). Long-haul and short-haul outbound all-inclusive package tours. *Asia Pacific Journal of Tourism Research, 9*(2), 161–176.

Lohmann, M., & Danielsson, J. (2001). Predicting travel patterns of senior citizens: How the past may provide a key to the future. *Journal of Vacation Marketing, 7*(4), 357–366.

Luborsky, M. R., & McMullen, C. K. (1999). Culture and aging. In J. C. Cavanaugh & S. K. Whitbourne (Eds.), *Gerontology: An interdisciplinary perspective* (pp. 65–90). New York, NY: Oxford University Press.

Metro Daily. (2009a, February 20). Hong Kong millionaire—Housewife come up second. Retrieved from http://www.metrohk.com.hk/index.php

Metro Daily. (2009b, February 18). Senior citizen has great market potential in cruise tourism. Retrieved from http://www.metrohk.com.hk/index.php

Milman, A. (1998). The impact of tourism and travel experience on senior travelers' psychological well-being. *Journal of Travel Research, 37*(2), 166–170.

Mok, C., & Armstrong, R. (1995). Leisure travel destination choice criteria of Hong Kong residents. *Journal of Travel & Tourism Marketing, 4*(1), 99–104.

Mok, C., & DeFranco, A. L. (1999). Chinese cultural values: Their implications for travel and tourism marketing. *Journal of Travel & Tourism Marketing, 8*(2), 99–114.

Muller, T. E., & O'Cass, A. (2001). Targeting the young at heart: Seeing senior vacationers the way they see themselves. *Journal of Vacation Marketing, 7*(4), 285–301.

Ng, E., Cassidy, F., & Brown, S. (2006, July). *An exploratory study on consumer travel agency information sources: An Australian regional analysis.* Paper presented at the International Conference on Business and Information, Singapore.

Patterson, I. (1996). *Growing older: Tourism and leisure behaviour of older adults.* Wallingford, England: CABI Publishing.

Pizam, A., & Jeong, G. H. (1996). Cross-cultural behavior: Perception of Korean tour guides. *Tourism Management, 4*(4), 277–286.

Plog, S. C. (2001). Why destination areas rise and fall in popularity. *Cornell Hotel & Restaurant Administration Quarterly, 42*(3), 13–16.

Qu, H., & Wong, E. Y. P. (1999). A service performance model of Hong Kong cruise travelers' motivation factors and satisfaction. *Tourism Management, 20*(2), 237–244.

Reimer, G. D. (1990). Package dreams: Canadian tour operators at work. *Annals of Tourism Research, 17*(4), 501–512.

Richardson, S. L., & Crompton, J. (1988). Vacation patterns of French and English Canadians. *Annals of Tourism Research, 15*(4), 430–448.

Shoemaker, S. (1989). Segmentation of the senior pleasure travel market. *Journal of Travel Research, 27*(3), 14–21.

Shoemaker, S. (2000). Segmenting the mature market: 10 years later. *Journal of Travel Research, 39*(1), 11–26.

Sirakaya, E., & Woodside, A. G. (2005). Building and testing theories of decision making by travelers. *Tourism Management, 26*(6), 815–832.

Tan, E. S. (1981). Culture-bound syndromes among overseas Chinese. In A. Kleinman & T. Y. Lin (Eds.), *Normal and abnormal behaviour in Chinese Culture* (pp. 371–386). Dordrecht, The Netherlands: D. Reidel Publishing Company.

Travel Industry Council of Hong Kong. (2009). *Find a travel agent.* Retrieved from http://www.tichk.org/public/website/en/index.html

Tsang, E. W. K. (2001). Internationalizing the family firm: A case study of a Chinese family business. *Journal of Small Business Management, 39*(1), 88–93.

Tsang, N. K. F. (2011). Dimensions of Chinese culture values in relation to service provision in hospitality and tourism industry. *International Journal of Hospitality Management, 30*(3), 670–679.

Tse, D. K., Belk, R. W., & Zhou, N. (1989). Becoming a consumer society: A longitudinal and cross-cultural content analysis of print ads from Hong Kong, the People's Republic of China, and Taiwan. *The Journal of Consumer Research, 15*(4), 457–472.

United Nations. (2002). *World population ageing 1950–2050.* Retrieved from http://www.un.org/en/index.shtml

Wang, K. C., Chen, J. S., & Chou, S. H. (2007). Senior tourists' purchasing decisions in group package tour. *Anatolia, 18*(1), 139–154.

Wang, Y. (2005). *An exploratory study on travel constructs in mature tourism* (Doctoral dissertation). Available from ProQuest Dissertations and Theses Database. (Accession Order No. 3183178)

Wong, S., & Lau, E. (2001). Understanding the behavior of Hong Kong Chinese tourists on group tour packages. *Journal of Travel Research, 40*(1), 57–67.

World Tourism Organization. (2001). *Tourism 2020 vision: Global forecasts and profiles of market segments.* Retrieved from http://www.unwto.org/index.php

Xing, F. (1995). The Chinese cultural system: Implications for cross-cultural management. *SAM Advanced Management Journal, 60*(1), 14–20.

Yavas, U. (1987). Foreign travel behavior in a growing vacation market: Implications for tourism marketers. *European Journal of Marketing, 21*(5), 57–69.

Yuan, S., & McDonald, C. (1990). Motivational determinates of international pleasure time. *Journal of Travel Research, 29*(1), 42–44.

Zhang, H. Q., & Lam, T. (1999). An analysis of mainland Chinese visitors' motivations to visit Hong Kong. *Tourism Management, 20*(5), 587–593.

Zimmer, Z., Brayley, R. E., & Searle, M. S. (1995). Whether to go and where to go: Identification of important influences on seniors' decisions to travel. *Journal of Travel Research, 33*(3), 3–10.

Index

Note: Page numbers in **bold** type refer to figures
Page numbers in *italic* type refer to tables

Aaker, J.L. 78
Ahluwalia, R.: Swaminathan, V. and Stilley, K.M. 80
American Traveller Survey 5
Anderson, B.: and Langmeyer, L. 99
Anderson, J.C.: and Gerbing, D.W. 82
animal behavior 41
annoyance: evaluation 51–5; level *52–3*; level and behavior types *48–9*
annoying behaviors: Macao 39–56
Ap, J. 26
attributes 9
Australia 21
average variances extracted (AVEs) 27

Baloglu, S.: Millar, M. and Kneesel, E. 79; Sirakaya-Turk, E. and Ekinci, Y. 76; and Usakli, A. 76, 79, 81
barriers: language 33, 36; travel 96–7
Basu, K.: and Dick, A.S. 78, 80
Beerli, A.: *et al* 77, 79, 88; and Martín, J.D. 81
behavior: annoying in Macao 39–56; issues 40–1, *see also* tourist behavior study
Bennett, M.J. 65
Blackden, P. 40
Bond, M.H. 100

Caltabiano, M.L.: and Pearce, P. 7
careers: travel 5, 7–8
Carr, N.: and Li, J.W.J. 21
Chen, C.F.: and Tsai, D. 78
Chen, J.L.: *et al* 17–36
Chi, C.G-Q.: and Qu, H. 81
competence: intercultural 61–72
conceptual model 9–11, *10*
consequences 10

consumer satisfaction (CS) 19–20, 21
coordinated management of meaning (CMM) 41
Crompton, J.L. 6, 77
Crosno, J.L.: Henard, J.H. and Freling, T.H. 78
cross-cultural interaction: and intercultural competence 64–6
cruise ship industry 98–9
cultural difference 36, 65; coping with 65

Danielsson, J.: and Lohman, M. 109
Dann, G. 5, 42; push and pull theory 5–7
DeFranco, A.L.: and Mok, C. 105
departures: outbound 4–5, **4**
destination image 75–90; role 77–9
destination loyalty 75–90; and self-congruity 79–80
destination personality 76, 78–9; and self-congruity 79–80
Dick, A.S.: and Basu, K. 78, 80
Ding, P.: *et al* 3–13
discrimination: anticipated 64; in marketplace 63–4; perceived 64; research 63, *see also* Hong Kong discrimination study

Ekinci, Y. 79; *et al* 79–80; Sirakaya-Turk, E. and Baloglu, S. 76
Enoch, Y. 98, 103
Epoch Times 95
escaping and seeking theory 5–6
expectancy-disconfirmation model 20
expectancy-value theory: and MEC theory 8
Expedia 40

farms *see* Taiwan recreation farms study
Fodness, D.: function theory 5, 8
Forbes, L.P.: and Freling, T.H. 78

Freling, T.H.: Crosno, J.L. and Henard, J.H. 78; and Forbes, L.P. 78
Fuchs, M.: and Weiermair, K. 34
function theory 5, 8

Gartner, W.C.: and Tasci, A.D.A. 78
Gerbing, D.W.: and Anderson, J.C. 82
Go, F.M.: Kumar, K. and Govers, R. 78
Goh, H.: and Litvin, S. 79
Govers, R.: et al 80, 89; Go, F.M. and Kumar, K. 78
Guens, M.: Weijters, B. and Wulf, K.D. 78
Guttman, J.: and Reynolds, T.J. 8

Helgeson, G.J.: and Supphellen, M. 80, 81
Henard, J.H.: Freling, T.H. and Crosno, J.L. 78
Heung, V.C.S. 21
Hofstede, G. 100
Hong Kong: Basic Law 71; Bill of Rights Ordinance 71; hypothesized tourist satisfaction model 25; millionaires 95; outbound tourism development 95; population growth 95; Race Discrimination Ordinance 71–2; sector-level satisfaction model 31; tourists 17–36; TSI 21, 33; TSI model 22; -UK TSI comparison 34–5, 35; -UK TSI difference statistical test 34
Hong Kong discrimination study 61–72; characteristics of respondents 67–8; descriptive statistics 68–9; descriptive statistics and reliability 69; grouping 69; MANCOVA 69; MANCOVA results 70; methodology 66; results 67–70
Hong Kong senior citizens study 94–110; Chinese cultural influences 100; data analysis 101–2; data collection 101; directions for future research 109–10; discussion 102–8; importance 102–5; instrument design 101; IPA 106–8; limitations 109–10; methodology 100–2; outbound package tours 105; package tours 97–8; performance attribute ranking 102–5; preferred mode of travel 98–9; respondents demographic information 103; results 102–8; sampling 101; travel agency performance 105; travel barriers 96–7; travel characteristics 99–100, 102, 104; travel motivations 96–7
Hosany, S.: et al 78–9
Hruschka, H.: and Mazanec, J. 107
Hsu, C.H.C.: et al 96
Huang, S.: and Hsu, C.H.C. 62
Hung, K. 1

importance-performance analysis (IPA) 106–8; grid 107
intercultural competence 61–72; concept 62; and cross-cultural interaction 64–6
Iso-Ahola, S.E.: escaping and seeking theory 5–6; and Mannell, R.C. 5–6

Jang, S.: and Wu, C.M.E. 7, 103–4
Javalgi, R.: et al 98
Jiang, S.: et al 1–13
Johar, J.S.: et al 79

Kau, A.K.: and Lim, P.S. 21
Kennedy, A.: and Ward, C. 66
Kneesel, E.: Baloglu, S. and Millar, M. 79; et al 89
Kressmann, F.: et al 76, 77, 79
Kumar, K.: Govers, R. and Go, F.M. 78

laddering 3, 8–9, 11, 12, 13; interview process 11; soft 11
Langmeyer, L.: and Anderson, B. 99
language barriers 33, 36
Lee, D-J.: et al 79
Lee, L.Y-S.: et al 94–110
Lee, U-L.: and Pearce, P. 7–8
leisure farms see Taiwan recreation farms study
leisure travel 4
Li, G.: et al 17–36
Li, J.W.J.: and Carr, N. 21
Li, L.: and Qu, H. 21
Li, X. (Robert) 1
Lim, P.S.: and Kau, A.K. 21
Lin, C.H.: et al 78, 88; and Morais, D.B. 89
Lin, W-R.: Wang, Y-C. and Liu, C-R. 75–90
Littrell, M.: et al 99
Litvin, S.: and Goh, H. 79
Liu, C-R.: Lin, W-R. and Wang, Y-C. 75–90
Lo, A.S.Y.: et al 94–110
Lohman, M.: and Danielsson, J. 109
Loi, K.I.: and Pearce, P. 39–56
loyalty: destination 75–90

Macao: host perspectives in 39–56; tourist perspectives in 39–56
McDonald, C.: and Yuan, S. 6
Mannell, R.C.: escaping and seeking theory 5–6; and Iso-Ahola, S.E. 5–6
marketplace: discrimination 63–4
Martín, J.D.: and Beerli, A. 81
Maslow, A.H.: motivation theory 7
Mason, M.F.: and Morris, M.W. 42
Mazanec, J.: and Hruschka, H. 107

means-end chain (MEC) theory 3–13; as conceptual model 9–11, *10*; expectancy-value theory 8–9; implications 11–12; laddering technique 3, 8–9, 11, 12, 13; six-level model **9**

Melton, A.W. 41

Millar, M.: Kneesel, E. and Baloglu, S. 79

millionaires 95

Millman, A. 96

Mo, X.: and Ryan, C. 21

Mok, C.: and DeFranco, A.L. 105

Morais, D.B.: and Lin, C.H. 89

Morris, M.W.: and Mason, M.F. 42

motivation *see* tourist motivation

Muller, T.E.: and O'Cass, A. 97, 99

multivariate analysis of covariance (MANCOVA) 69, *70*

New Zealand 21

O'Cass, A.: and Muller, T.E. 97, 99

Oliver, R.L.: expectancy-disconfirmation model 20

outbound departures 4–5, **4**, *see also* package tours

outbound tourism 18; Hong Kong development 95

package tours 97–8, *105*; senior citizen selection 94–110; service quality 65–6

Patterson, I. 97

Pearce, P. 5, 12, 64; and Caltabiano, M.L. 7; and Lee, U-L. 7–8; and Loi, K.I. 39–56

people watching 41

personality: destination 76, 79–80

Philipp, S.F. 63

Pike, S. 76

Pizam, A.: *et al* 42; and Sussman, S. 42

Plog, S.C. 5

psychocentric-allocentric model 5

purchasing power 4

push and pull theory 5–7

Qu, H.: and Chi, C.G-Q. 81; and Li, L. 21

recreation farms 76; Yilan Shangrila 80, 88, *see also* Taiwan recreation farms study

Reisinger, Y.: and Turner, L.W. 62, 64

Reynolds, T.J.: and Guttman, J. 8

Ryan, C. 7; and Mo, X. 21

satisfaction *see* Tourist Satisfaction Index (TSI) study

Scott, N.: *et al* 3–13

self-concept 77

self-congruity 76, 77, 89; destination loyalty 79–80; destination personality 79–80

self-image: actual/social/ideal/ideal social 77

senior citizens *see* Hong Kong senior citizens study

senior travelers **97**

service quality: tours 65–6

Shanghai: purchasing power 4

Shoemaker, S. 99

Singapore 21

Sirakaya-Turk, E.: Baloglu, S. and Ekinci, Y. 76

Sirgy, M.J. 77: *et al* 79, 81; and Su, C. 76, 79, 81

Sociocultural Adaption Scale (SCAS) 66

Song, H.: *et al* 17–36

Stilley, K.M.: Ahluwalia, R. and Swaminathan, V. 80

structrual equation models (SEMs) 23

Su, C.: and Sirgy, M.J. 76, 79, 81

Supphellen, M.: and Helgeson, G.J. 80, 81

Sussman, S.: and Pizam, A. 42

Swaminathan, V.: Stilley, K.M. and Ahluwalia, R. 80

Taiwan Leisure Farms Development 81

Taiwan recreation farms study 75–90; —data collection 80–1; discriminant validity test results *85*; Hypothesis 5 results *87*; measurement 81–2; measurement model analysis results *83–4*; path analysis of indirect effects *86*; path analysis of research framework *86*; results 82–7; sample 80–1; structural equation model path analysis **86**; structural model analysis results *85*

Taiwanese Leisure Farm 81

Taiwanese Recreation Farming Development Association 76

Tasci, A.D.A.: and Gartner, W.C. 78

Tidwell, J.: *et al* 79

tourism motivation 96–7: conceptual model **10**; consequences 10; values 10

tourism motivation theories 5–8; escaping and seeking theory 6; functional theory 8; push and pull theory 6–7; psychocentric-allocentric model 5; TCL 7–8; TCP 7–8

tourist behavior 40, *see also* annoying behavior

tourist behavior study 1, 42, 43–55; analysis 46–55; annoyance evaluation 51–5; demographics of respondents *45–6*; demographics of sample 44–6; discussion 46–55; frequency evaluation 51–5;

frequency-annoyance grid **50**, **51**; general frequency-annoyance evaluation 47–50; instrumentation 44; intergroup comparison 50–1; intergroup comparison of frequency *52–3*; level of annoyance *52–3*; level of annoyance of tourist behavior types *48–9*; literature review 41–3; mean scores of frequency *48–9*; methodology 43–6; new categorical themes 50–1; results 46–55; sampling 43–4

tourist satisfaction (TS) 20; hypothesized model **25**

Tourist Satisfaction Index (TSI) study 17–36; analysis 23–35; AVE of estimated models *27*; computation of overall destination TSIs 29; computation of sectoral TSIs 29–33; Cronbach's Alphas *27*; demographic profiles 24–5; destination satisfaction analysis 25; framework 21; Hong Kong computed sectoral/overall *33*; Hong Kong sector-level satisfaction model **31**; Hong Kong tourist satisfaction model **28**; Hong Kong tourists 17–36; Hong Kong-UK TSI comparison 34, **35**; Hong Kong-UK TSI difference statistical test *34*; language barriers 33; methodology 22–3; model **22**; model fit 26–8; model reduction 25–6; multiple R2 *27*; reliability 26–8; results 23–35; sector-level satisfaction model **30**; structural relationships 29; survey respondents profile *24*; UK computed sectoral/overall *33*; UK sector-level satisfaction model **32**; UK tourist satisfaction model **28**; UK tourists 17–36

tours: selection 94–110; service quality 65–6

travel agency performance *105*

travel barriers 96–7

travel career ladder (TCL) 7–8

travel career pattern (TCP) 5, 7–8

travel characteristics: Hong Kong senior citizens 99–100, 102, *104*

travel motivations: Hong Kong senior citizens study 96–7

travelers, senior **97**, *see also* Hong Kong senior citizens study

Tsai, D.: and Chen, C.F. 78

Tsai, H.: *et al* 94–110

Tsang, N.K.F. 100; *et al* 94–110

Turner, L.W.: and Reisinger, Y. 62, 64

United Kingdom (UK): Chinese outbound tourism 19; -Hong Kong TSI comparison 33, 34–5, **35**; -Hong Kong TSI difference statistical test *34*; overall TSIs 33; sector-level satisfaction model **32**; tourist satisfaction model **26**, **28**; tourists 17–36; VisitBritain 19

Usakli, A.: and Baloglu, S. 76, 79, 81

Uysal, M.: and Yoon, Y. 20

values 10; personal 12

VisitBritain: Chinese outbound tourism 19

Walsh, G. 64

Wang, Y. 96; *et al* 21

Wang, Y-C.: Liu, C-R. and Lin, W-R. 75–90

Ward, C.: and Kennedy, A. 66

Weiermair, K.: and Fuchs, M. 34

Weijters, B.: Wulf, K.D. and Guens, M. 78

Witt, C.A.: and Wright, P.L. 7

World Tourism Organization (UNWTO) 1; Tourism Vision 2020 Report (1999) 18

Wright, P.L.: and Witt, C.A. 7

Wu, C.M.E.: and Jang, S. 7, 103–4

Wu, D.C.: *et al* 17–36

Wulf, K.D.: Guens, M. and Weijters, B. 78

Ye, H.B.: Zhang, H.Q. and Yuen, P.P. 61–72

Yilan Shangrila Recreation Farm 80, 88

Yoon, Y.: and Uysal, M. 20

Yuan, S.: and McDonald, C. 6

Yuen, P.P.: Ye, H.B. and Zhang, H.Q. 61–72

Zhang, H.Q.: Yuen, P.P. and Ye, H.B. 61–72

Zou, T.T. 3–13

For Product Safety Concerns and Information please contact our EU
representative GPSR@taylorandfrancis.com Taylor & Francis Verlag GmbH,
Kaufingerstraße 24, 80331 München, Germany

Printed and bound by CPI Group (UK) Ltd, Croydon, CR0 4YY
01/05/2025
01858357-0006